PRAYER POWER

CW01572561

OTHER BOOKS BY MELVIN BANKS

Healing Secrets
The Greatest Miracle of All
Power for Living
Is Anything Too Hard for God?
Wind of Fire
With God All Things are Possible
Expect a Miracle
Lay Hold of God's Power

PRAYER POWER

How God Can Act In Your Life

Melvin Banks

Marshall Pickering
An Imprint of HarperCollins*Publishers*

Marshall Pickering is an Imprint of
HarperCollins*Religious*
Part of HarperCollins*Publishers*
77–85 Fulham Palace Road
London W6 8JB

First published in Great Britain
in 1997 by Marshall Pickering

1   3   5   7   9   10   8   6   4   2

Copyright © 1997 Melvin Banks

A catalogue record for this book is
available from the British Library

0 551 031239

Printed and bound in Great Britain by
Caledonian International Book Manufacturing Ltd, Glasgow

Contents

– 1 –

The Power of God's Call

'All the days of my service I would wait
until my release should come. You would
call, and I would answer you.'

JOB 14:14–15

I awoke early to a knock on the door, and shouted out
my usual greeting to the day: 'Praise the Lord!' Yet
another exciting day, I thought. Bridget, the hostess
looking after me in Luton, brought in my morning cup
of Earl Grey tea. 'By the way,' she said, as she left the
room, 'the pastor rang up urgently to chat with you,
but he said he'd call back later.'

Just minor arrangements, I thought, musing on the
busy and challenging day ahead of me: two services,
morning prayer *and* a healing session in the afternoon,
which the BBC was coming to film for its local evening
news programme. With over four million viewers, what
an opportunity to spread the Good News of the Gospel!

I began to get ready and, as always, knelt down to
pray. I had not been on my knees long when there was
another tap on the door. It was Bridget again, to tell me
that George, the pastor and organizer of the events, was
actually on his way to see me. I still wasn't at all
perturbed – I thought it was just the finer points of the
day that he'd want to finalize. Or maybe he wanted to
talk again about the fantastic service we'd held the

night before at his church – a good crowd turned out, 17 people were born again, many were filled with the Holy Spirit and even more were healed. What inspiration this was, as I continued to work on the two sermons I was due to preach later that afternoon and evening. I was so engrossed in my work, that I didn't even hear the doorbell ringing.

It was only when I heard the voice of the pastor calling upstairs, saying, 'Come down, I need to see you urgently!' that I remembered he was coming to see me. I got to my feet, put on my tie, straightened it, slipped into my cosy slippers, and stepped downstairs – little did I know it, to a new destiny ...

I met George in the passageway. His voice sounded grave, and he seemed mysteriously subdued – secretive, almost. He ushered me into the spacious, comfortable front room, and Bridget made a hurried, silent departure. As he sat down and motioned me to do the same, I finally knew that something was brewing. The George who sat opposite me wasn't the normal, buoyant, bright, positive George that I knew. He was shaking, trembling, fidgeting with his hands – almost unable to look me in the eye for more than a moment.

Slowly, he began to open up to me. 'I could not sleep a wink last night, not a wink,' he stuttered. 'I'm sure it was God, He doesn't speak to me so forcibly, Melvin.'

I leant back in my chair, intrigued as to what I was about to hear.

'Many years ago,' George continued, 'He spoke to me and I didn't listen. I spent eight years in the wilderness, out of touch with God, all because I refused to listen to what He was saying to me.'

'But what has this got to do with me, George?' I demanded. 'We've got a great day ahead of us – there's so much to do for Jesus.'

'This has everything to do with you,' he answered. 'God was speaking to me about you.'

'Have I done something wrong?' I asked, aghast.

'No, Melvin,' he reassured me. 'Everyone went away from last night's service thrilled and happy. It was an excellent evening, it couldn't have been better. I've nothing to complain about – God has blessed you. But …' – he went on, almost whispering – 'but last night God told me …' – a silent gap followed as he swallowed and could hardly get his words out – '… He told me that you must pack your bags and go straight home!'

I was stunned. In all my years of ministry, never before had a minister advised me to do such a thing. I was instantly suspicious.

'Are you sure I haven't offended you, or that there's something you're not telling me?' I insisted.

'No,' George stated firmly, 'it's the truth. God has only spoken to me in this way a few times in thirty years of work for Him. He's always been right, though. Melvin, God says that you *must* go home.'

I couldn't believe it. Here was a man I trusted like few others, a man of great character, an anointed pastor and friend, one not given to extraordinary visions or out-of-body experiences, down-to-earth, honest – a good man. He had looked forward to this crusade for many months, had spent a great deal of money, advertised, prepared … and here he was telling me to return home!

I began to remonstrate. 'What about my name and character? People will say that I've fled, that I'm losing my head, that I've become unreliable.'

George looked at me and said quietly, 'Melvin, if God is asking you to do this, then He will take care of you. Your good name will only be enhanced.'

I tried one last time. 'Let me go in a few hours after the BBC has filmed. Let's not miss reaching millions with the Gospel.'

'Melvin,' George replied adamantly, 'God said to go home now. Don't stop for anything – go *now*!'

An hour and a half later I was packed up and back on the road. Lilian, my wife, welcomed me home. She was certainly startled – in 34 years as an evangelist's wife, she'd never known her husband to come home two days and three services earlier than planned!

The only way to begin to understand what God intended for me was to spend time alone with Him. I've never carried out any work for God without first really feeling His call to me. I would not have dared lift a Bible to preach, or lay a hand on a sick person, or even enter a church, unless God Himself had spoken to me.

I knew that I needed to feel the conviction of God's plan for me, so for four days, I shut myself off from the outside world – no television, no phone calls, no interviews, no press, no counselling, no formal prayer sessions. Just me, four walls, a closed door, my Bible and God. I didn't see a great light, there were no appearances of angels – in fact, nothing extraordinary at all; all I felt was fear, awe, wonder, brokenness and blind faith as I asked of God: 'What next?'

I was able to take reassurance from those wonderful words from Paul's letter to the Hebrews: 'Let us be brave, then, and come forward to God's throne, where there is grace. There we will receive mercy and find grace to help us just when we need it' (4:16).

Marvellous Manifestations

When I had completed my four days with God, a good part of the time in fasting, I still didn't have the answer I was waiting for. On the Friday, Lilian reminded me I was preaching that night in the East End of London, with a further couple of services on Saturday and Sunday. 'Oh, and by the way,' she added, 'it's a small church. You're only starting with about six people ...'

It was only when I stood there in the church, that I felt I was beginning to understand God's message for me. I'd been concentrating so much on the thought that *millions* could be reached, that I'd overlooked the importance of *local* revival. God's first sign to me was to make me realize the importance and impact of starting small, and seeing how things could increase from there.

Going by the hundreds of services I'd carried out in the past, it was an exceptionally small group I preached to on that first evening. As it turned out, a few more than the predicted six people had come along, and the church was busy and full of noise and anticipation by the time the service started.

God, you are doing something new here, I thought. Most people hadn't even been to a Christian service before, so I immediately set about teaching them a few hymns and Gospel songs. They loved them! So many of them then responded to my salvation invitation, after I spoke about the power of the Blood of Christ to save our souls. They'd no idea that you could actually know God personally.

To speak to so many and win so many was amazing. And as if that wasn't enough, the next day we were to see many healed or helped through their sicknesses by prayer, in the name of Jesus Christ. A young Irish lady brought her eight-year-old deaf son, Shaun, to the service. By the end, he could hear perfectly. He, and over 150 other people, were healed and brought to Christ. It was revival indeed! By the Sunday evening, we were seeing amazing things happening. Shaun's mother went out into her local Irish community, telling them of God's wonders. She brought 72 new people on the Sunday evening to the service to hear the Gospel. Most of those 72 – including three tough boxers – were converted or healed that night, *or both*! Like ripples on a pond that spread further and further outwards after only a single stone has been thrown in, so this one person was able to lead several others to Christ. From small beginnings ...

COME AND EMPTY THE HOSPITAL!

That month, October 1995, was definitely turning out to be a remarkable time for me. Soon after that wonderful experience in the East End, I received a call from a doctor in the south of England, who asked me to visit and pray for the patients of a large private hospice of which he was head doctor. Of course, I'd been to hundreds of hospitals to pray for individuals at their or their families' request. But here was an actual meeting inside the medical centre. The last time I'd taken a service in a place like this was for carol singing when I was a young pastor, but no one got up from their wheelchairs and walked home then!

The very first lady I laid hands on that afternoon was affected by a bad stroke. After much prayer she lifted her dead arm, used her paralysed hand for the first time since the attack, smiled, spoke and walked! It brought the place down! We may not have seen the Lord empty the place, but many were blessed, and no one will ever forget the miracle of that lady. That evening, about 400 people crowded into the largest public building in the town. Someone said afterwards that they'd never seen such a response to conversion – prayer went on until 11.30 p.m., 110 people were born again, many others walked, took off neck braces, ran without pain or regained their hearing. I thanked God for the new anointing He was giving – the tide was rising, God was doing something because of my new-found obedience to Him.

'In Dublin's Fair City'

Later that same month, Lilian and I flew into Dublin for another crusade. It was a bright, sunny morning. We were whisked through the airport facilities into a waiting car by Harry and Maureen, two of the organizers. They were tremendously excited, believing that revival was about to break out, and they were full of stories about various arrangements, the huge number of phone calls they'd received about the event, and sick people even being brought from hospitals to be healed.

We were using the Regency hotel, on the main road into Dublin. It was perfect, with a large hall and excellent facilities. The owners kindly let it to us at the lowest price possible, all because it was for God's work. On the first night, 400 people came – a modest number, but for Dublin, a great crowd. Power swept the building. I told the people, 'It's not a disgrace to come to Jesus, but a grace!' In three nights, 350 people were born again, many seized by the anointing of the Holy Spirit in unusual ways. People were gripped by spiritual intensity: a blind girl could see the spots on my tie; a daughter, with tears streaming down her cheeks, was thrilled to see her elderly mother get up from her wheelchair and – for the first time in years – walk yard after yard, metre after metre; a woman who had been using a crutch after an awful accident, and who was in agonizing pain, actually began to run up and down! She returned the following night fit and well, with no pain and no crutch, giving her testimony to the crowd. It was the first time ever she had spoken in a religious or church meeting publicly. The *Irish Herald* ran a full-page feature about the crusade, bringing it to the attention of a huge section of Ireland's population. Here in Dublin I vividly saw the ongoing fruit of what God had set aside for me to do.

FILLED WITH THE SPIRIT

On my return from Dublin, I'd set aside a few days for some well-earned rest, but it wasn't to be! Almost immediately I was travelling across the North Sea to Holland. I'd visited this lovely country some seven years previously, and had led many successful crusades.

On my tour, I visited a church near Maastricht. The young pastor there was relatively new; on his arrival, sadly, many folk had left and he subsequently became discouraged with no tangible evidence of his message being heard and acted upon. However, when I met him, he'd just returned from Toronto, where he and his wife had a remarkable awakening and rich personal blessing in its ongoing revival. They brought that revival to the remnants of their church, and every member had been richly endowed with fresh impetus, joy, zeal and release in the Holy Spirit. As a result they were one in the Spirit; a new basis had been founded on God's Word.

During the meetings while I was there, approximately 40 new people joined the church. A man left his wheelchair, someone else threw away his crutches and began to walk, whole families came to the Lord – the church was in transformation. There was noise, cries of relief and excitement, joy, laughter, tears, walking miracles, salvation. To some, it may have appeared irreverent – shambolic, almost – but God loved it, the Holy Spirit was there. He set the people free to receive all His gifts and endowments. As is written in the Acts of the Apostles, as the Holy Spirit came down, there were *more* evangelists, not less!

What did this new blessing mean to me? It seemed as if God was taking the challenge even higher, He was hitting hitherto unproductive places, He was breaking down tough, fallow ground – He was using me to send the light to even further unreached territory. I was now listening to God even more intently. There was also a tenderness, a sweetness, a graciousness, a deep love of the Holy Spirit. This is the difference that I have felt from that day in Luton when God transported me and I obeyed – reluctantly!

GOD'S CALL TO YOU

God's call to each and every one of us is personal. He knows what we're about. On a friend's desk is a motto: 'I am glad to think I am not bound to make the world go right, but only to discover and to do with cheerful heart the work that God appoints.' It's a quotation by Jean Ingelow, and every time I read it, it challenges and cheers me. It prompts me to trust God and remember that His call for me is the right one, even when I think it isn't! In any walk of life, there are enough obstacles to be overcome and victories to be won, without us looking around at work we are not suited for. I think this story tells it beautifully.

Years ago, a violet grew near the trunk of a tree. The violet was modest. The tree was proud.

'You poor little, helpless, useless thing,' said the tree contemptuously. 'You'll bloom and fade within a few days. But look at me. I'll stand here for centuries. You are weak, I am strong. You're worth nothing; I'm of great value. Don't you feel miserable about it?'

'Frankly, no,' said the violet. 'I can't be a tree, however much I want to be. So I'm content to be a violet. Anyway, folk say I'm rather sweet.'

That very day, a flash of lightning shattered the proud tree. After the storm, in the quietness of dusk, a woman walked that way. She was a mother who had lost her child. She saw the violet, plucked it, carried it home and pressed it between the pages of her Bible. And there it is still, bringing comfort to her daily.

To work out God's call for you may be very difficult. It needs great patience and lots of prayer. Even when you do discover what His call is, it may be hard to face! You may be impatient to get things done, and as a result get over-anxious and worn down. 'The most unhappy man is he that is not patient in adversity, for men are not killed with the adversities they have but with the impatience they suffer.' That bold statement was written centuries ago on the wall of a cell in the Tower of London. The writing is still clear and the truth shines as brightly now as ever. Be patient! By staying calm you'll be surprised how much more you can achieve. The old lines are true:

> The calling seems impossible,
> A task too big for you;
> You know it's much too hard,
> A job you just can't do!
> But here's the wonder and surprise,
> Amazing and yet true,
> You can do what's impossible,
> And do it finely, too!

God will use you as *He* wills. Step back, and ask yourself, 'Am I doing God's will? Am I following His purpose?' Are you ready? Could you change every plan, no matter how good and godly it seems, and follow God's call? Jesus is the maker of men. He said, 'Follow me and I will make you fishers of men' (Matthew 4:19). Simon and Andrew, fishing on Lake Galilee when Jesus said this to them, left all they had, obeyed His call, and followed Him. Are you prepared to do the same? Would you be willing to drop everything – even the chance to minister to millions for Christ, as I had to – just to hear God speak? It takes some doing, as I found out, but it is worth it. As St Paul wrote: '… but rather surrender yourselves fully to God' (Romans 6:13). As one door shuts, so another opens. Be ready to accept the challenge!

– 2 –

MIRACLES IN ABUNDANCE!

> So they remained for a long time, speaking
> boldly for the Lord, who testified to the
> word of his grace by granting signs and
> wonders to be done through them.
>
> ACTS 14:3

As I enter a town or city on the way to one of our crusades or services, I always claim God's words to Paul in the Acts of the Apostles: 'I have much people in this city.' The local press, television and radio stations are usually there, and the cry rings out: 'Mr Miracle is here – show us your miracles!' There's often upheaval, there's always a challenge, but the Lord sees us through.

MIRACLES ON AIR

I'll always remember the first time Lilian and I went to New Zealand, and the particularly inspirational crusade which I led there in Auckland. Looking back at the events of the time I was there proves more than ever before that through prayer, God *does* answer our questions and solve our problems – in this instance, miraculously so!

I had come to New Zealand at the invitation of Pastor John Coleman, leader of a church of 150 people. My ministry was quite unknown there. Auckland, while perhaps not as vast as other great cities of the world was, nevertheless, a needy city. I had prayed for it much in recent months as I travelled through England, my thoughts often turning to my forthcoming visit to this beautiful country. Now, having arrived in New Zealand, I needed prayer more than ever before – I was facing an enormous challenge.

On my arrival, John had explained to me about an event he'd helped to organize with Radio Pacific – a national radio station – which had the potential to spread the Good News across the whole country. I was about to make New Zealand media history by going on the famous 'Mike Baker Show' to pray publicly for the healing of the sick. Some weeks before the programme, the producers had issued an announcement inviting any sick and incurable people to come onto the programme and be prayed for by me, 'the English evangelist'. They were overwhelmed by the response and, from the huge number of applications, eventually chose five very sick people.

The station authorities were well aware of the genuine sickness of the people selected, and the idea was that I should not meet them until the actual programme, which was to go out 'live'. They announced that I would be laying hands on these people, using phrases like 'to see if it's genuine' and 'if there's anything in it'. I knew I was facing a barrage of scepticism.

So, after the first meetings of the crusade, which had attracted good sized congregations, I made an urgent call to my British crusade organizer, and to my personal secretary, asking them to pray and to organize intercession for me back in Britain. I really didn't know what I was letting myself in for.

On the way to the station that morning, even the taxi driver knew all about the programme!

'If ever you needed a miracle it's today,' he said solemnly as he negotiated the early morning rush-hour traffic of the city. I reclined in the back seat, watching as the colonial-style wooden buildings of the suburbs gave way to the shining glass and tower blocks of the city.

'We are really up against it today, Melvin,' he went on. 'Nothing like this has ever been attempted here before on the media.'

I gulped an acknowledgement, feeling rather like an innocent victim pressed into taking someone else's place on the guillotine. A car horn beeped behind us; an ambulance siren wailed in the distance, taking some casualty to hospital. I might be a casualty myself by the end of the morning, I reflected nervously.

Walking through the swing doors of Radio Pacific, I reflected on what Daniel must have felt going into the lions' den. I had not boasted of my ministry; I had never, at any time, claimed to do anything in *my* power. However, the reputation I had gained during all my years of ministry in Britain was enough to make me a target for sceptics, eager to expose anything about my ministry that was not genuine. The people at the radio station did not believe in my ministry, and I knew that they hoped to catch me out and prove that I could not produce the goods. They were not dishonest or corrupt people, but were approaching the issue in the only way that they knew.

I shook hands with the producer, his assistant, the technicians and the interviewer, and could sense their hesitation. But as I sat waiting to be introduced on to the programme, praying quietly, the Spirit of the Lord arose in my being with an anointing such as I had not felt for many years.

Although I must have been praying only for moments, I was so lost in God that it seemed like an age, and I was quite oblivious to all that was taking place around me. I was brought back to earth with the noise of a door shutting and a voice saying, 'Coffee, Reverend Banks?'

'Pardon?'

'Coffee? Oh, are you all right?'

'Yes, I'm all right. No coffee, thanks.'

'We're ready for you now,' said the assistant, and my thoughts flew to my darling wife Lilian, who was fasting and praying in our lodgings at the other end of the city. Pastor Coleman told me later that many pastors were listening all around Auckland, and in one church four pastors sat huddled around the set awaiting the annihilation of this funny little Englishman who had dared to 'take on the NZ broadcasting set-up'. There were some who had said that I was crazy to presume on God and risk the good name of the Evangelical Church in the country, and put so much at stake. It was just as well I did not know all that was being said about me, as New Zealand's most popular morning programme, broadcast from end to end in the two islands, was about to begin.

I made myself comfortable in the chair opposite the interviewer, and looked through the glass panelling at the engineers' tuning equipment and at the producer and two other staff members walking around shuffling papers and talking. The red light came on.

'This is Radio Pacific and this is the moment you have all been waiting for. We have here in our studios the healing evangelist from the United Kingdom, the Reverend Melvin Banks, on his first visit to New Zealand. He's holding healing services in Glendene, here in Auckland.' Mike Baker then went on to announce the names of the five people who'd come in to the studio to be healed.

I felt humbled and quietened, but in my heart came a voice:

> *The Kingdom of God is within you. Preach the Gospel of the Kingdom and heal the sick. My Kingdom is in you; my power is in you; it is not you, but I who will defend my Word. I will work such a work that many will wonder ... remember you have the power of the Kingdom in you!*

I felt such confidence, such boldness arising in me. The anointing was upon me; I was the King's representative, the ambassador of the King of Kings!

The first of the sick people came to face me. She was crippled in her shoulders and spine, paralysed by arthritis and a form of spondylitis. She was racked with pain and her body had been seized up for 14 years. I laid hands on her and prayed. I felt power surging into her beyond myself. She began to cry out, 'Oh, it's wonderful! It's wonderful! Look at that!' and she sat up, moved her shoulders briskly, and bent her spine. Then she was dancing round the studio! She could bend, she could jump, her rigid neck was free, all her pain had disappeared, she could do the impossible!

Baker began to get very excited as he delivered his commentary. 'We know all about this woman,' he began. 'She has not moved like this for years! Mr Banks has never met her before – this is amazing!'

Then, one after the other, the sick people were brought in, and God healed four of them. The fifth, though not healed, was greatly helped and comforted and felt some improvement, so was also very joyful. The studio became like the scene of a revival meeting. People were praising God, the staff were visibly flabbergasted, the switchboard was jammed with telephone calls and people began to arrive at the studio wanting prayer. Announcements were hastily made: 'Please do not come to the studio, but go to see the evangelist at the big marquee in Glendene.'

Then one of the studio staff came in. This was an associate producer who had previously totally rejected the idea of Christ's healing power. Now he came to ask me if I would pray for him. He had pulled a muscle 18 months before, and had suffered ever since from constant, nagging pain, which no medical help had been able to alleviate. I laid hands on him and he too was instantly and miraculously healed – and all this broadcast 'live' from the studio!

At last, after a gruelling three-hour session of answering phone-in calls, responding to the interviewer's questions, praying and seeing miracles, I left the studio on the best possible terms with the station staff, and with many newly-made sympathizers from all over New Zealand.

At our subsequent public meetings held each evening, the crowds grew to over 1,000 people, and when an overflow system was organized, we were seeing congregations of 1,500. We had to move to a huge church building in the city centre as the crowds continued to grow and grow, until thousands had been reached with the Gospel of Christ. It was the same in the other cities we visited: Christchurch, Wellington, Whangarei. Crowds packed the largest halls; in a month some 4,000 came to Christ and 10,000 came forward for healing prayer. Amazing miracles were seen! Pastor John Coleman said, 'It touched every part of our nation of New Zealand, with a dynamic effect on the non-churchgoing public ... not seen here for 60 years since the visit of the old healing evangelists Valdez and Smith Wigglesworth; thousands healed, vast numbers turned to Christ.'

On my second trip to New Zealand, some thirteen months later, I returned to Radio Pacific with John Coleman. As we parked the car, Mike Baker was looking out of his office window. He recognized me straightaway and waved enthusiastically. Travelling up to the studio in the lift, a well-dressed, healthy-looking man smiled at me. He looked familiar but I couldn't place him. Later, John Coleman reminded me. He was the studio producer who was initially sceptical of my ministry, but who then had come forward for healing himself. (Mike was later to tell me that since I prayed for this man, he'd never experienced the same pain again.)

We sat in Mike's spacious but untidy office. A secretary popped in. 'The phones are ringing already,' she announced. 'It's going to be a busy morning!'

Mike introduced the phone-in session. 'Great to see you here again, Melvin,' he began. I recalled his reserve, caution – cynicism, even – on my first visit. Now what smiles, what enthusiasm! He explained that they had checked up on the different cases I had prayed for after I had gone. Indeed, a follow-up programme showed them to be extremely positive in their new-found health. I was delighted when Mike continued, 'We are going to speak to them all again today, to see how they're doing. The last I heard, they were full of life ...'

He was to use that phrase often during the next three hours. Hundreds of calls came in, and the producer asked if I could stay on the phone-in for another hour, which I gladly did. Mike talked to four of the people who had been in the studio the previous year and it was wonderful to hear their stories. Joy had come to their families, they could walk again, go out shopping, work, help their children. Each one used phrases like 'I have an entirely different life now' or 'I am totally different since this experience' or 'I have begun to live life again!'

It was marvellous to realize that people were receiving *life*, not only in great public healing meetings, in evangelism services and individual counselling groups, but also in a busy, national radio station, crammed with worldwide news of despair, riot, coups, corruption, violence, war, disease, famine and trouble. God was there in all the hurly-burly.

With God, Nothing is Impossible

Jesus answered the man, 'If thou canst believe, all things are possible to him that believeth.'

MARK 9:23

A producer from BBC 2 rang me recently saying that they were intending to make a programme about miracles, and the Assemblies of God headquarters had given my name as the best person to contact. 'I'll do what I can to help,' I chuckled, 'but Jesus is the man you must contact if you want some miracles!' I went on to describe case after case of healing miracles, which the producer found incredible – unbelievable, even. But what she didn't realize was that what appeared seemingly impossible to her was nothing to the Almighty; God is so big, so strong and so mighty, there's nothing that He cannot do!

In the Acts of the Apostles, we read of Peter preaching to the crowds about Jesus, talking about the proof of His Messiahship. 'Jesus of Nazareth,' he said, 'a man approved of by God, among you by miracles and signs and wonders, which God did by him in the midst of you' (Acts 2:22).

Jesus didn't just perform miracles to order, as if they were mere displays of His power. Rather, they were simply evidence of who He actually was; they were the signs and seals of His mission. People saw their own sinfulness, they saw themselves as they really were against the miraculous revelation of the divine and supernatural being of God in Christ. The miracles of Christ forced the message of God on to the people.

Harold Horton once said: 'Miracles are the golden bow that in God's purpose fling the arrow of the Gospel.'

The *Oxford English Dictionary* defines a miracle as 'anything beyond human power and deviating from common action of the law of nature'. C. S. Lewis described it as 'an interference with nature by supernatural power'. St Augustine said, 'I should not be a Christian but for the miracles.' I have been tremendously blessed: I have seen incredible miracles, extraordinary miracles, stunning miracles! They've certainly shown to me the explosive power of God – and I hope that you'll think so too.

I conducted a mission in the French city of Nancy, a great metropolis of some 250,000 people but with only three small evangelical churches. The Assemblies of God church was the largest of these, with about eighty members. Its pastor, though, had faith; he booked a five-hundred-seater hall for the mission with only about 30 to 40 workers to help. The first night about 150 came, among them many sick people. One group consisted of Turkish Muslims, who had never been in a Christian meeting in their lives. The local government officials provided an interpreter to sit with them and I also had a French interpreter on the platform with me, so we had two translators for the two different groups. God anointed my message as I preached of the 'one Saviour for all mankind'. Many signified they would like to know Jesus at the close of the meeting when we had a time of counselling.

Afterwards, there was time set aside for laying on of hands for the sick. Among the folk who came forward were a number of the Turkish group, including a little boy who was deaf and dumb; in fact, he'd never spoken in his life. As I touched the boy I asked Jesus to reveal Himself as the living God of love. As I prayed, the little boy looked up and turned his head all around. He put his hands over his ears because the noise of people praying just overcame him. We tried speaking the alphabet to him, and then through the interpreter asked him to respond to the language of his parents. Soon they were actually communicating with him and he began to utter letters and words in Turkish. It was clearly a startling miracle for everyone and many asked for more prayers and help. The following evenings' meetings were crammed full with people coming to hear more about God. Why had it happened? I believe it was because God knew it was a place of need and so placed His gift amongst them.

On another crusade in France, around 1500 people were coming each day to the meetings. A young woman carried her son to the hall; he had a growth on his knee and could not even stand up. It was likely that he would have to undergo an amputation. But, after praying for him, there was a transformation. Two weeks later, the boy was running about as his mother described how he had been discharged from the hospital – he was completely cured.

A short time ago, I held a healing service in a Northamptonshire town. A woman had brought her profoundly deaf granddaughter for prayer, but because the hall was so crowded, they could not get inside and so had to stand outside during the service. She later testified that as I was praying for the sick, she felt a sense of awe, wonder and divine glow. A flow of power seemed to shoot through the building, and at that moment the child began to clutch her ears tightly. She could hear the traffic on the main road; she could hear the praise and clapping of the people in the hall. A miracle indeed!

I must tell you about my old friend Bert in Portsmouth. He really is a living testimony to the miraculous power of Christ today. Bert was a heavy drinker; he spent his days in the pub and believed in nothing – not even himself. One evening his wife announced that she was going out. Bert was puzzled, since she tended to be a homebird who rarely went out by herself. It turned out she'd received a pamphlet through the door about a crusade I was leading, and wanted to see for herself what it was all about. Bert laughed and went off to the pub, but when he arrived home that night, he found his wife joyful and singing hymns. The same thing happened every night that week. Bert was mystified by the change in his wife, yet he resisted all her attempts to persuade him to come to a meeting.

At last the crusade ended and I moved on to another town. But Bert's wife had bought one of the tapes that had been on sale at the crusade, one by Alan Pimlott, the renowned soloist from Norwich. She played this wonderful tape non-stop! Bert heard it when he got up in the morning, he heard it when he came home from the pub each night. Finally, he really began to listen to it. The message in the songs started to make sense. Eventually, he asked his wife if he could accompany her to the local Christian Fellowship she had begun to attend. Two of the elders prayed for Bert and he was converted. A lifetime's habit of heavy drinking stopped – he was free!

Another mission I held was in a mining community extremely affected by the recent mine closures. They were rough, tough, sceptical people, very hard hit by recession. Yet, as the local newspapers all testify, sensational scenes took place as people flocked to the services. The bingo hall manageress was quoted as saying 'I may as well close up – I've done virtually no business while all this has been going on!' Police had to be called out to control the traffic because crowds of people were travelling from around the area to attend the services. That was a miracle for today!

I think of David, from Reading. When I was asked to pray for him, he was unable to talk, he pulled himself around on his stomach, he could hardly feel his legs and the hospital had warned him that he might never walk. Within three months of that prayer he was standing, and within a month he was walking. He is now a completely normal, fit and healthy teenager.

After witnessing miracles such as these, my faith is immensely stronger and I yearn to see yet more outpourings of God's Spirit. But, as always, we must start by praying; with God, nothing is impossible, but nothing is possible without prayer. These poignant words encapsulate what I feel:

> I want to scale the utmost height
> And catch a glimpse of glory bright;
> But still I'll pray till heaven I've found.
> Lord, lead me on to higher ground.

– 3 –

PRAY AT ALL TIMES

> Do not worry about anything, but in
> everything by prayer and supplication with
> thanksgiving let your requests be made
> known to God.
>
> PHILIPPIANS 4:6

My early days of ministry began in the Salvation Army, from where I really began to learn the discipline of prayer. I've got old Alfred Cox to thank for that! Alfred, a life-long Salvationist, took me under his wing as a new convert. If for any reason I missed the 7.30 a.m. prayer meetings – called 'knee drill' in those days – I would soon have old 'Coxy' after me! He would place his hand on my shoulder, and gently explain to me that my place was in the prayer meetings. Old Alfred was severe, sour at times, but strict in his prayer times. I certainly learnt an important lesson in that early discipline.

Although we need to discipline ourselves to pray each day to God, it needn't be a severe discipline. Daily prayer will soon develop into a joyous discovery which enables us to learn more about ourselves and God. The practice and art of prayer must be foremost on our list of spiritual priorities. Reservoirs of power are at our disposal – but only as we pray. The main direction of faith is to enable us to exercise a successful prayer life. It is more important to pray than to worship, even. It brings us under the Lordship of Christ in our communion with Him, and it keeps us in the Holy place of continuous yielding, brokenness unto the Living God.

I always find that I am able to meet the day with confidence when I have spent time with God. It sets me up for the day – I feel I can tackle anything! It's so important that both individually and corporately we rediscover the value and power of prayer; for both individual and corporate life, like a watch, has a tendency to run down.

WHY PRAY?

Hear my prayer, O Lord;
let my cry for help come to you.
Do not hide your face from me when I am in distress.
Turn your ear to me;
when I call, answer me quickly.

PSALM 102:1–2

Do any of these statements ring true with you?

- How can praying possibly help me out of my mess or dilemma?
- I get nothing out of prayer.
- In my experience, the end is no different from the beginning.
- I can't cope with the discipline of prayer, but the Lord knows how busy I am.
- I don't see the point of prayer. It's such hard work, and other things grab me more.
- I don't believe God needs me to tell Him what to do.

- I feel so unanswered in prayer, usually when I'm most desperate for something to happen.
- My mind always wanders when I pray, let alone when you lead us in church.
- I'm not sure I believe anyone is really there, or else he's too remote for people like me.
- It's like phoning Directory Enquiries and being told your call is stored in the queue, but you never reach the front of the queue before you ring off, either in frustration or in despair.
- I reckon I'm more likely to win the National Lottery than I am to hit the jackpot in prayer.

I'm sure you'll have heard – or said – some of them before! It's precisely at times like these that we need to remember that the Holy Spirit is there to help us be bold in prayer. He strengthens our faith. For example, if you want to buy some exotic fruit but doubt that the greengrocer sells what you want, you will probably say: 'I don't suppose, by any chance, that you sell mangoes?' or 'You wouldn't sell mangoes, would you?' These words show that you are almost embarrassed to be asking for something so outrageous as mangoes! The shop assistant sees your diffidence and doesn't hesitate to tell you there are no mangoes today and that you're welcome to try somewhere else for such an odd request!

But if you shop boldly – 'I want a couple of mangoes; I gather this is a good place to buy them' – the assistant notes your confidence, and thinks twice about letting you down. Do you see what this says about faith? The Holy Spirit helps us to be bold in prayer. He stirs us to 'go for it'. He strengthens our faith so that we keep praying, even when we're tempted to doubt and to stop.

THE PRACTICE OF PRAYER

Many Christians expect results without any practice of the art. A little boy who heard someone play 'God save the Queen' on a mouth organ at a fairground bought one, and when he got home and failed to get a tune out of it, burst into tears and told his mother: 'The man cheated me, there is no "God save the Queen" in this mouth organ.' Many of us just as foolishly believe we can get ready-made spiritual results without the practice of prayer. Would we not think a person foolish who played a musical instrument only occasionally, expecting to tune in to music and become the instrument of music without taking time to practise? If we spent half as much time in learning the art of prayer as we do in learning any other art, we would get ten times the results.

Some people, you see, use God just like little Mary did just before her holidays. Mary was only four and every night at bedtime she knelt to pray under the watchful eye of her mother. The night before the annual family holiday, Mary said her prayers as usual, but after completing them she remained on her knees. There was a momentary silence, and then she said, 'Goodbye God. You won't be hearing from me for the next four weeks, I'm going on my holidays.' We can't stop praying just because our daily routine is altered – we should continue to fit God into our lives no matter where we are or what we are doing. A friend's young son was intrigued by the fact that God is everywhere. One day, when they were alone, he asked: 'Can God see us?' When his mother said 'yes', he asked: 'Can He see us now?' She gently replied: 'Yes, God can see us.' To her amusement he ran behind the settee saying: 'Come on, let's hide!' God is with us at all times, so we don't need to feel that we can pray only at certain times.

Other people are like the fighter pilot in the RAF, who, while walking across the tarmac, was asked by the chaplain if he ever prayed. 'Oh yes,' the pilot replied, 'I pray when I'm flying.'

'But I never see you in my chapel services,' the chaplain continued.

'Oh no, when I'm on the ground I can manage myself!'

These people think that it's only in an emergency that we need to pray – when something is needed, or when a particular problem needs solving. But God wants us to pray to Him whatever our situation, in good times and in bad times. 'Whether it is good or evil, we will obey the voice of the Lord our God ... that it may be well with us ...' (Jeremiah 42:1–22). Prayer should be constant. We should pray at all times in the Spirit.

Still others think that prayer is like the amazing new tractor seen at an agricultural show recently. With the touch of just one button, the tractor went up and down the field, pulling the plough behind it; it ploughed the whole field, released the plough, left the field, went up the country road, turned into the farm and put itself away in the barn. The farmer didn't even have to get out of bed! And this was all the result of a press of a button.

People presume that God is a press-button God: one touch and He'll do it all, with no cost, no sacrifice and no fuss. How wrong they are! Prayer takes hard work and sacrifice on our part – only then will we see the glorious results.

LEARN BY LISTENING

A young woman on the verge of a breakdown was told by her doctor: 'Jane, I don't know what to do for you. You had better go home and get on your knees and pray.' Surprising advice for a general practitioner to give, some might think! When the girl returned home, she told her mother what the doctor had said and asked: 'Mother, don't you think it was a strange thing for him to say?' Her mother said, 'Yes, it was, but why don't you try it?' Jane did and within an hour was a new person. The doctor was gloriously in the Spirit in the girl's case – it was the right diagnosis and the right prescription. At the end of her tether, what Jane needed was to take time out to be with God and listen to what He had to say.

That's probably the most important point – to *listen*. To grow as Christians we must learn to listen to God, not just to talk at Him. Like all communication, prayer is a two-way process – we talk to God, and He listens; He talks to us, and we listen. Prayer is a *dialogue*, not a monologue. You could begin your prayers by reciting this simple verse:

O Father, as I kneel in Your presence today, help me to realize that prayer is not just me speaking

to You, but You speaking to me. Speak to me
today, in the same clear way that You spoke to
Your Son. For His dear Name's sake I ask it.
Amen.

If we don't approach God with the right attitude – that
of listening – we will gradually not even be able to hear
His voice, and spiritual paralysis will set in.

A minister stood up in a small prayer meeting some
years ago and said: 'God has shown me tonight that I
must shift the emphasis in my life from talking to
thinking.' He had caught on to one of the greatest
lessons in the Christian life – receptivity. 'Then Samuel
said, "Speak, for your servant is listening" '(1 Samuel
3:1–19).

I am amazed at how many Christians I meet who,
when I ask them about their prayer life, tell me that
although they spend a lot of time talking to God, they
rarely pause to let God talk to them. One of the best
pieces of advice I ever received was from a man who
said: 'After you have talked to God in prayer, relax and
say to Him, "Father, have you anything to say to me?"
Then just listen.' Prime the pump of your spirit and get
in the mood for prayer; give God an opportunity to illu-
minate some word or passage to your heart and thus
make you aware of His personal interest in your affairs.

Christians who lose touch with their faith do so
primarily because they have failed to establish and
maintain clear lines of communication with God. They
do not listen. A church poster I saw the other day put it:
'If at this moment God seems far away – guess who
moved?!' Prayer and the neglect of it is one of the prime

reasons behind spiritual defection. The less we pray, the less motivated we will be to live and behave as a Christian should. 'I've let down on my prayer time,' said a missionary to me the other day, 'and I'm suffering defeat after defeat in my Christian life.' Is it any wonder?

I love this verse by Ethel Roming Fuller about the two-way communication we have with God:

If radio's slim fingers can pluck a melody from night,
And toss it over a continent or sea;
If the petalled white notes of a violin are blown
    across the mountains or the city din;
If songs, like crimsoned roses, are culled from thin
    blue air,
Why should mortals wonder if God speaks in prayer?

Once you've opened up the lines of communication with God once more and have begun to talk to Him – and listen to Him – in prayer, pour out before Him all your feelings: the discouragement, the doubts, the despair. Hold nothing back. The more real and honest you are, the more God can do for you. Martin Luther once said: 'The first rule of prayer is to be honest.' That's certainly the case! Experience has shown that something happens when a person is honest with God.

AN ANSWER TO A PRAYER?

If we want something, we should ask for it, right? Well, yes – but God doesn't always see it like that! We don't always get what we want, and perhaps we're not asking for the right things. A preacher tells of a woman who told him she was leaving the church and never returning. When he asked why, she said that her daughter had sat for a scholarship, and although she and her little girl had prayed hard, she hadn't passed. Indeed, not only that, but she had come bottom of the list. That proved, the mother claimed, there was nothing in prayer, and because of that she was not attending church any more. The preacher concluded: 'It struck me as I listened to her that I had not taught her much about prayer.' He knew the daughter well and realized that achieving a scholarship was perhaps not the best thing for her in the long run. Perhaps the wrong prayers were being asked! We shouldn't be like that actress, Mae West, who said 'When I'm caught between two evils, I take the one I've never tried.' We must only take, ask and seek after what is helpful, wholesome and purifying for us.

Someone once said to me, 'When the conditions are right, God does not say "yes" to our prayers. He is not really saying "no" – He never says "no" – it's just that He doesn't say "yes" when the idea is not the best for us!'

He does not say 'yes' when the idea is absolutely wrong for us; He does not say 'yes' when it may help you, but create problems for others. The Bible makes it clear that God does not answer all selfish, begging, childish, crying and pitiful pleadings. Some have totally selfish, materialistic and cynical prayers. Prayer is not a scream or a scheme to get things. It is a relationship with God, which fosters a growth of spirituality, a spiritual exercise whereby we draw ourselves to God, where we can get into closer harmony with God's great plan and purpose and peace for us. Prayer is not always to give you what you want, but instead to turn you into the person God wants you to be.

Recently I asked a little boy in a wheelchair what he would like to be when he grew up. He cocked his head and furrowed his brow in deep thought. I was expecting an answer such as 'I want to be a fireman' or 'I want to be a jet pilot' (disabled kids don't let wheelchairs get in the way of their dreams) but this child's answer took me by surprise. With the most gentle of smiles he said: 'When I grow up I want to be like Jesus.' Isn't that the dream of us all? How wonderful it would be if that dream were realized as we grew up – perhaps we could start now by understanding that this is what God wants for us too.

Those who find the idea of listening for God's voice in prayer too challenging should remember that this is not the only way God speaks. He also communicates to us by quickening our hearts to some word or passage of Scripture. That is why it is important to have a Bible close at hand when you pray. Ideally, it is best to begin your prayer time with the Bible and also to end with it. Beginning with the Bible helps. Perhaps you could pray something like this: 'Forgive me, dear Lord, that my prayer life is built around the attitude, "Listen, Lord, Your servant is speaking" rather than "Speak Lord, Your servant is listening". Help me to get my attitude right – today. In Jesus's Name. Amen.'

POWER THROUGH PRAYER

God's power really does come through prayer to us. The motto outside a church in Missouri, USA, reads: 'We believe that the power behind us is greater than the task before us!' Dr Cho recently arrived at the First Baptist Church, Dallas, Texas, to preach at the Sunday morning service. It was held at 8.00 a.m., but he'd arrived – along with his brother and assistant, Cha – at 7.15 a.m. They were both invited to join the earlier prayer meeting, to which they heartily agreed. Brother Cha couldn't help but point out that Dr Cho had already spent three hours in prayer before that prayer meeting and subsequent service had begun – imagine the immense power that was on Dr Cho as he preached to the vast crowd that morning!

Prayer gives us surviving power. To survive in this world of ours, with its constant media bombardment, attacks on morals and justice, and pressure to conform to our peers, we can learn to get by with prayer. We need to meditate, to turn over in our minds all that God asks of us, to think of the Scriptures and the thoughts of God.

A prayerful man was once asked: 'Do you count sheep to go to sleep?' He replied, 'No ... I talk to the shepherd!' As you speak to and share with Jesus in prayer, you'll sleep even better as well. When I'm far away from loved ones, and lay my head down to sleep – perhaps in the heart of south-east Asia, bitten by fifteen mosquitoes a night and with lizards running over my bed, or with mice under the bed in Belgium, or the cry of the Mullahs at 5.00 a.m. in the Middle East calling the Muslims to prayer, or at 700 mph in jumbo jets, or in the shunting, creaking, overnight trains from the north of Scotland, or in the back of cars driven over mountain roads in the South of France – if I make sure I take time to pray, I seem to be able to sleep anywhere on my travels for Jesus!

Prayer is life-changing and life-creating. All the great Christian leaders of the past have been men and women of prayer. John Wesley once declared, 'God does nothing but in answer to prayer,' and backed up his belief by devoting two hours a day to the sacred exercise. The great Methodist preacher, Dr W. E. Sangster, once wrote: 'Part of the secret of progress in the spiritual life is to harness the mind in prayer in the quest for Christ.'

'Where your treasure is there your heart will be also' (Matthew 6:21, NIV). Your treasure must be in Christ – wholly and supremely – let it be speaking to Him and receiving from Him in prayer. Often circumstances of life get people into an attitude of readiness for praying. Look at Habakkuk's response in the Old Testament. In his third chapter, he begins by requesting divine mercy: 'Lord,' he says, 'I have heard of your fame, I stand in awe of your deeds, O Lord. Renew them in our day, in our time make them known, in wrath remember mercy' (3:2). Then Habakkuk proceeds to pray for his beleaguered people. The Babylonians are bearing down on them, tragedy is inevitable. Confronted with the whole situation, the prophet prays and pleads for divine mercy. Then he carefully recounts divine history. He remembers what God has done and stands on His goodness.

Moses prayed for the people: 'Don't let them be lost. Blot me out of your book ... but save them.' What passion, what praying! Moses gave them a chance, he stood in the gap and was willing to suffer himself so that others' needs might be met: 'Save them, give them a chance, blot me out instead of them,' he cried. We need to plead with God, weep rivers of tears from the depths of our souls like this.

PARTNERS IN PRAYER

In all of my prayers for all of you, I always pray with joy because of your partnership in the Gospel from the first day until now.

PHILIPPIANS 1:4–5

J. Edgar Hoover commented: 'The spectacle of a nation praying is more awe-inspiring that the explosion of an atomic bomb.' I feel that one of the keys to God working out His plans is Christians in prayer partnership. The Scriptures make a strong plea for Christians to be partners, no matter what pressure they may face. 'But that its parts should have equal concern for each other. If one part suffers, each part suffers with it' (1 Corinthians 12:25–26). We are exhorted to mourn with those who mourn (Romans 12:15) and share each other's burdens (Galatians 6:2). When Christians do come together in partnership, unity and earnestness, incredible things can happen. And when God sees us completing our side of the bargain, as it were, then He can really start making things happen. As Oswald Smith put it: 'When we work, we work, when we pray, God works!'

By working hard at our prayers God answers us – and he really does want to answer us. He said to Abraham: 'Shall I hide from Abraham what I want to do?' (Genesis 18:17). God wants to inspire us in prayer. There is such a satisfaction in prayer, such a joy in waiting for God. 'If my people shall humble themselves, pray, seek my face ... then will I hear from heaven ... and heal their land ...' (2 Chronicles 7:14).

In the next chapter I'll talk about how we can concentrate our whole being in order to pray successfully. Now, reflect on the list below, and see what a difference praying can make!

- Prayer makes the shallow soul – deep.
- Prayer makes the foolish – wise.
- Prayer makes the ignorant – intelligent.
- Prayer makes the slothful – busy.
- Prayer makes the weak – strong.
- Prayer makes the indifferent – zealous.
- Prayer makes the unbeliever – trustful.
- Prayer makes the craven – courageous.

– 4 –

PREPARE TO CONCENTRATE

> ... thou incline thine ear unto wisdom, and
> thine heart to understanding ...
>
> PROVERBS 2:2

Each time I visit my wife's family in Tyneside, I never cease to be amazed at the fact that the teapot is always kept warm. You don't have to say 'Put the kettle on' – it's *always* on! The kind-hearted welcome with which we are received into their home never changes either. Just like the kettle, the warmth within them is constantly bubbling away! I like to compare this to our prayer life. We must always keep our minds fixed and our hearts galvanized so that we are ready to pray – to talk *and* listen to God – at any time. In the words of Psalm 57, 'My heart is fixed, O God ... fixed, I will give praise, awake myself, awake early, I will praise thee among the people.'

'But I just can't concentrate,' so many people tell me. 'What should I do?' I know what they mean – it happens to me as well! I begin to pray, but my mind wanders mercilessly, thinking of the priorities for the week ahead, the appointments to fulfil, the phone calls to make and the post I must answer. It's often a real struggle for me to focus my mind, and I find I have to capture each wandering thought and bring it back into submission for the task of prayer! Then I find that I can't focus on anything specific to pray for, since some areas like 'for the poor' or 'for Africa' seem too broad. Sometimes, I simply feel that I'm no good at prayer.

Inevitably, it's St Paul who shows us the way forward. 'I will pray with my spirit, but *I will pray also with my mind*' (1 Corinthians 14:15). It's so important to remember that prayer is not simply a gabble of hurried words and phrases – the pauses can be as significant as the words themselves. Prayer is not just idle chatter – it demands concentration. Prayer doesn't just happen, it entails the engaging of the mind as well as the spirit. It's not the length or the poetic phraseology of our prayers which is important, but their sincerity and simplicity. As Jesus said, 'When you pray, do not use a lot of meaningless words, as the pagans do, who think that their gods will hear them because their prayers are long. Do not be like them. Your Father already knows what you need before you ask him' (Matthew 6:7–8). Rather, true prayer comes from clear thoughts which have been carefully formed in the mind. In short, prayer needs work!

CONCENTRATION PAYS OFF

The story of Gladys Aylward – the famed missionary to China – shows how important it is to concentrate and listen to God's Word in your life.

In 1966, it was my wife's privilege to hear Gladys speak at a meeting held during her final visit to England. That simple, God-filled talk in the Baptist Church in Skegness was unforgettable to Lilian. Aylward was a woman who had learnt to concentrate –

indeed, it revolutionized her whole life. As a young woman in her early twenties, she knew that God was calling her to China, a land of rebellions, violence and poverty. Everyone discouraged her from going – friends, her church, acquaintances – all thought her either quite unsuitable, or just plain mad! Only her parents believed in her mission. It took her years to save up the fare, but on 15 October 1930 she set out on her incredible journey with only £2 in her pocket and a case with Oxo cubes and tins of corned beef and sardines. She travelled on the Trans-Siberian Railway across Russia (and through a local civil war!) into Manchuria, and finally into China.

Aylward had actually been turned down for missionary work by the notable missionary society, the China Island Mission, who thought she was unsuitable. But that didn't stop her! She kept praying, learnt to concentrate her thoughts on God and thus find out His mind, will and purposes, and became a resounding success. For 40 years she spread the Gospel of Christ to untold thousands of Mandarin people. She fed the poor, brought hope to the heartless and miracles to many unbelievers. She saved 100 orphans during the Japanese War, and later set up an orphanage; literally, it was heaven on earth for count-less children. There is no doubt that the great revival in China today can be partly attributed to her ministry and sacrifice. Her story is now known to millions across the globe. She's been to Buckingham Palace to meet the Queen, and has met numerous Heads of State during her world tours. She died at her orphanage in Taiwan at the age of 68, having brought comfort, warmth and food to so many orphans. Her story is an inspiration to us all.

Planning Pays Off

Over the years, I've gradually learnt how to concentrate when I pray – with the help of God, of course! (And it's not easy to concentrate when you're battling to pray alongside the cry of wild parrots in the jungles of Asia, the call of the kangaroo and the jackal in the Australian outback, the shout of the Mullahs from the Islamic towers in Malaysia, the drone of the noise of traffic in New York and Tokyo, the squawks of the penguins and seagulls in the Falklands, the sound of helicopters in Northern Ireland and tornadoes in India – all of which I've experienced during my time of ministry!)

Here's my five-point plan to aid you in your prayer life: isolation, revolution, co-ordination, co-operation and revelation.

1 Isolation

Spend a little while alone with God, just with a chapter of the Bible in front of you. Read it several times, even if you don't understand it perfectly, or even if your mind is wandering. Repeat to yourself: 'I will not leave this room until I concentrate on God!' Isolate yourself until you begin to see and understand.

I'm not talking about self-seeking or selfishness here, though. Isolation does not mean the big 'I'. Don't let isolation cut you off from the whole purpose of the Christian life, why you are searching for more of the

Holy Spirit and why you are meditating on His divine Word: not for self, but for His name and His glory.

It's no easy task to rest your mind, at times it will feel like a battlefield. But to give up and lose the fight is to wander, to miss God's oft-quiet voice, to be cheated out of His will and your own personal happiness ... so much can be lost when we don't win in concentration. Be ready to battle!

2 Revolution

Be willing to have a personal revolution in your life-style. Some things will have to change if you are to move on to higher places in your spiritual walk. Hindrances to your concentration will have to be dealt with. Be practical. Set aside a definite time for God amidst the rush and bustle of your life – and stick to it; even a little time can bring rich rewards!

With this revolution, though, don't be too harsh; do what you know you can do, and don't make unfeasible demands on yourself. I'm reminded of the story of a born-again Christian who went to his doctor and complained, 'I've got a persistent headache that won't go away.'

'Do you smoke?' asked the doctor.

'No.'

'Drink?'

'No.'

'Go dancing?'

'No.'

'Socialize?'

'No.'

The doctor thought for a moment and said, 'I think I know what's wrong with you. Your halo is too tight!'

The key here is to be relaxed and enjoy Jesus. I still enjoy every moment of work: my preaching, meditations, reading the Word, helping people, praying for the sick, bringing comfort to people. Making a change in your life is hard, but can be done. Listen to what God is calling you to do, concentrate and find out. Remember Gladys Aylward – she was revolutionized by listening to God and saying 'yes' to His call.

3 Co-ordination

God is always there to help us. Once you've set out on your spiritual journey, remember to co-ordinate with Him. Don't over-reach yourself and find that you are so frustrated that you are tense, and can't concentrate on prayer. Take a step at a time with God: 'The counsel of the Lord standeth forever, the thoughts of His heart to all generations' (Psalm 33:11).

David Copperfield said, 'Whatever I've done, I've tried to do it well, and have tried always to complete it.' We must also give all we can, and be intertwined with our Maker, seeking Him, having an aim. By co-ordinating with God, by coming alongside Him, we will be able to pursue our goal.

We recently had satellite television installed, as I wanted to be able to receive the Christian programmes that are now available (and the Disney Channel too!). The engineer told me that the satellite dish he'd been told to install would never work, and that I needed a better one. I held firm. 'This will do,' I said. And it did –

it worked perfectly. But note: the beam had to point in the right direction. Are you pointing towards God, are you co-ordinating with the Master? Here's a good example of co-ordination at work, when God speaks to Malachi: 'You bring all the tithes (of money, time, talent) into the storehouse, and I will pour you out a blessing that there will not be room to receive it. I will open the windows of heaven and flood you out a blessing' (Malachi 3:10).

4 Co-operation

Sam Waller built a $15 billion shopping empire in the USA; his stores – 'Wal-Marts' – are in every town. As his chain grew, he regularly kept in touch with all his staff, asking what they felt would sell better, what they suggested would improve their sales, etc. No wonder he was so successful! Sam Waller listened, talked and co-operated.

I am able to concentrate much better after I've discussed my thoughts and ideas with my team and my fellow pastors. We talk, we listen, we change things when necessary. My friend Debbie Curtis tells of an afternoon when her younger sister telephoned her. 'I'm having a dinner party tomorrow,' she said, 'but I can't decide what to cook.' Debbie gave her some simple recipes but was surprised that she hadn't contacted their elder sister, who was an excellent cook. When she asked why, the younger sister replied, 'Because I knew that if you could make it, I could!'

We cannot adequately concentrate until we are in harmony with our fellow believers, our church, our associates, our family. Sometimes, for example, I've had a bad misunderstanding with someone, and when I've been praying I just can't get any peace. My thoughts have always come back to this problem. Before I can return properly to my prayers, I have to go and heal the situation, sort it out. If you are failing to concentrate, why not look at your life and see if there are any areas where you need to co-operate more. Are there situations in which you need to hold out a hand of love and appreciation? Just watch the results if you do go and set things right – your mind will settle in no time!

5 Revelation

Sharpen your knowledge – faith is not so much inspiration as information. If we haven't got clear knowledge or direction, then it's so easy to become devoid of purpose or just plain lost. Don't sit back and be content with what you have. As you get more from God, and your appetite for knowledge increases, seek out more revelation. As Tennyson put it: 'The scholars outgrow their masters!'

In revelation there is concentration. There is nothing that keeps me longer in the prayer room, and at my Saviour's feet, then when He is telling me new things! Some people, however, are very insecure when receiving fresh revelation from God. They think that His Word is too much for them, and they're frightened that they might fail Him in His call. Other people simply feel wounded; they received revelation and tried to serve God through it, but gave up because it was too hard. Others are lazy. They don't give God's revelation the attention it deserves; all they want are the pleasures of life. Still others procrastinate, they put off acting on what's been revealed to them. It's never the right time, 'I'm not ready yet' is their favourite phrase.

All these responses are normal, but what we need to do is try to overcome them. Perhaps the key point to remember here is 'If God be for us, who can be against us?' (Romans 8:31). God will provide when we turn our lives and minds to Him.

Through listening to God's Word, concentrating and receiving knowledge, we will learn a great deal. Indeed, with faith in God – putting our trust in Him and obeying His call – confidence and victory will come our way. Having faith in God means: deciding to do something, before you can prove to yourself it will work; leaping blindly before knowing you'll make it; having to answer before you have all the facts; making a decision before you have solved all the problems and making a commitment before you can be absolutely sure you are making the right move. Not easy, is it? But give it all you have – this is the way to keep concentration uppermost, and not miss a thing God is saying. 'Jesus said, "Don't look for shortcuts to God, surefire, easygoing formulas for success. Don't fall for that. Crowds do. The way to life, to God, is vigorous and requires total attention [concentration]"' (Matthew 7:13, translation by Eugene H. Peterson in *The Message*).

GOD WILL PROVIDE

President Eisenhower told a story once in one of his speeches. An old farmer had a cow that a man wanted to buy. He visited the farmer and asked about the cow's pedigree. The farmer didn't know what pedigree meant, so the man then asked him about the cow's butterfat production. Again, the farmer said that he had no idea. So, finally, the man asked if the farmer knew how many litres of milk the cow produced each year. The farmer shook his head and said, 'I don't know. But she's an honest old cow and she'll give you all the milk she has!' Eisenhower then concluded his opening remarks, 'Well, I'm like the cow: I'll give you everything I have.'

God is the same. He'll give us everything He has. But we mustn't forget to keep praying. Jesus Himself often took time alone to pray. 'When He had sent them away, He departed to the mountain to pray' (Mark 6:46). I was preaching in Denver, Colorado a few years ago. What glorious scenery – beautiful white-capped, frosted mountains, the old cowboy country. There, they ride the extremely fast-flowing (and dangerous!) rapids. When a whitewater raft guide cries, 'Eddy out!' he doesn't mean 'Throw someone named Edward out of the boat'! Rather, it's the command for all the people on one side of the raft to hold their paddles against the current while the others stroke furiously. This turns the raft out of the swift water and into the quiet eddies along the river's edge. 'Shooting the rapids' is exciting but tiring. When the guide sees that everyone needs a break, he shouts 'Eddy out!' It's then time to pull along-side the shore into calmer waters, into safer havens, to recuperate, to reflect, to concentrate on the wonders around, to get ready for the next ride, the next wave of water.

In the same way, Jesus went from the pressure, the crowds, the demands, the sick, the doubt, the hopelessness, and had a breather. He reflected, He concentrated. Follow these methods, along with my five-point plan, and I know that eventually you will succeed in your prayers.

The victory in concentrating and leading on, perhaps even to miracles, is inside all of us. We must have faith and trust in God and we will receive the rewards. 'The Lord turned to him and said, "Go in this might of yours ... Surely I will be with you"' (Judges 6:14, 16).

I'll sum up with these inspirational words from the Dutch hymn writer, Van De Venter:

> All to Jesus I surrender,
> Lord I give myself to Thee;
> fill me with Thy love and power,
> let Thy blessing fall on me.

5

THE POWER OF WORDS

The sum of your word is truth;
and every one of your righteous ordinances
endures for ever.

PSALM 119:160

Shortly after Scottish preacher G. Campbell Morgan's wedding, his father visited the newly-weds' home, which they'd just furnished and decorated. Having shown him around with pride and satisfaction he remarked, 'Yes, it's very nice, but no one walking through here would know whether you belong to God or to the devil!' Morgan was shocked by his father's gruff but well-meaning comment. But he got the point. From that day forward he made certain that in every room of his house there was some evidence of their faith in Christ *in word*.

Just like Campbell Morgan, many Christians make an effort to include reminders of God's grace and goodness in their homes. A Bible verse inscribed on a plaque or a tasteful work of art with a Christian theme may be all that is needed to encourage family members to serve and praise the Lord. 'These words shall be in your heart …You shall write them on the doorpost of your house' (Deuteronomy 6:6, 9).

George Cole (you'll know him better as that likeable rogue, Arthur Daley, in the hit television series *Minder*) was once asked in an interview to name his favourite text from the Bible. He quietly replied that he had not been brought up to read the Bible, but during his early career as an actor, whilst staying at a backstreet boarding house, he remembered a landlady's text on her dining room wall: 'Jesus Christ – the same yesterday, today, forever'. He remembered it word for word 40 years later!

It just goes to show the immense power of the written word. Karl Marx, when asked how he would fuel the communist revolution, replied, 'with ink and a printing press!' Adolf Hitler was in prison when he wrote *Mein Kampf*, which ensured him an army of fanatical supporters. I visited Nuremberg recently, in the midst of a preaching tour. One of my hosts took me to the stadium used by Hitler for his great rally. I stood mesmerized by this huge edifice – now partly falling down – and realized that a million people had come here just to hear the words of this man. Our words certainly have the power to build up or to tear down.

THE BIBLE – GOD'S WORD

Smith Wigglesworth, that tremendous English preacher, under whose ministry 14 people were reportedly raised from the dead, once said 'I never consider myself thoroughly dressed unless I have my Testament in my pocket. I would as soon go out without my shoes as without my Bible!' In his travels all over the world, he stayed in many homes. People later reported that after every meal – even in restaurants – he would always push his chair back from the table, get out his

Testament and say, 'We have fed the body; now let's feed the inward man.' This echoes the words of Jesus when He said: 'Man shall not live by bread alone, but by every word that proceedeth out of the mouth of God' (Matthew 4:4).

What about us? Do we regularly read and study the Bible? It's never too late to find new wisdom in it. Even more importantly, it's never too late to start believing and obeying the Word of God which we find there. Many families pass treasured Bibles from one generation to the next as spiritual heirlooms. But these treasures are often treated as mere antiques: their pages go unread and their promises remain unclaimed. The message of salvation goes unheeded. The Bible's true value is thus never realized. We must remember, therefore, not simply to store the Bible on our shelf, but in our heart. The Bible is more than just a record of long-ago events and ancient wisdom. It is the Book that bears God's signature. It is His message of truth and grace to us. Let's not neglect it. Let's read it, believe it and obey it. I love this verse from Watts' poem:

> Great God, with wonder and with praise
> On all Thy works I look,
> But still Thy wisdom, power, and grace
> Shine brightest in Thy Book.

'No Man Can Tame the Tongue'

You can tame a tiger, a lion, a leopard, a cheetah and many other wild animals, especially if you work with them from their birth, but you can't tame the human tongue, according to the apostle James. He uses several vivid analogies in his writings to illustrate the enormous power of this little part of the body. A bit in a horse's mouth can turn the animal to the right or to the left (3:3). A ship's rudder can steer a huge vessel in a raging storm (3:4). A single match or even a small spark can start a fire that can destroy an entire forest (3:5). 'So it is with the tongue: small as it is, it can boast about great things' (3:5).

What James emphasizes is that words can be used for great things, but that we must be careful not to turn them to evil purpose. Even under the strictest self-discipline and constant monitoring, the tongue's unruly nature lurks dangerously below the surface. Hess wrote:

> Lord, set a watch upon my lips,
> My tongue control today;
> Help me evaluate each thought
> And guard each word I say.

Not only must we always aim to use our words to spread the Good News and to praise God and all His goodness, but to spread happiness and friendship amongst our neighbours. Wrong words, harsh words, unkind words and hurting words can all linger for many years, sometimes for all one's life. For example, Winston Churchill was continually haunted by his father's words when he was a boy: 'He'll never come to anything!' – he who later became one of the greatest orators and international leaders of this century. Another example: a cook in a noble house handed in her notice even though she was well-paid. When she was asked why, she replied, 'When the meal is good the Duke and Duchess never praise me; when it is bad they never blame me. It is just not worthwhile. Encouragement and rebuke would be so helpful.' A word in season would have saved her!

And, in a slightly different context, I can still remember the old saying on the posters at railway stations, on hoardings, in the Second World War – 'Careless talk costs lives!' Loving, tender and beautiful words, on the other hand, all sweeten, uplift, soften and change others around us. 'Pleasant words are as an honeycomb, sweet to the soul and health to the bones' (Proverbs 16:24).

Words, when used well, can have an immediate, important effect. For example, one morning on a train packed with businessmen and city gentlemen, three youths were seen with their cassette player, blaring out loud pop music. The din was deafening in the crowded carriage. One of the occupants shouted rather gruffly, 'Turn that stuff off!' but they only turned it up higher in response. Soon another, and another joined in, crying 'Switch off that racket!' The youths were oblivious to the situation, simply calling back 'We paid for our tickets too, we can do what we want!' The atmosphere was getting very tense. It was a few minutes later that the situation was resolved. 'Get that turned off or there will be trouble,' came a steady, calm, disciplined voice. Suddenly, the whole compartment went quiet. What made the difference? It was the voice of the guard. With his commanding authority and a few right words – spoken in the right way! – the problem was solved.

OUR WORDS ARE WITNESS

Nellie Pickard has written a series of books describing how she witnesses in everyday situations. In *Just Say It!* she describes a phone call she made to her local health-food store. On a previous visit, she had noticed that bee pollen was on sale, so she rang and asked the manager about the benefits of using it. 'You'll live for ever,' he assured her.

To Nellie, the words 'live for ever' were an open invitation. 'I know you're joking,' she said, 'but I know I'm going to live for ever, and not because I buy your bee pollen.'

His response was encouraging. 'I'd like to hear more about it,' he said, his attention well and truly grabbed. 'I'm really interested in why you think you're going to live for ever.' Although at that time he did not know Jesus as his Saviour, Nellie had planted the seed by being wise 'toward those who are outside' (Colossians 4:5).

I'm sure you've been in this kind of situation. An opportunity has arisen where a few choice words from us can open up all kinds of possibilities for talking about Jesus. And yet, how many of us have felt our words were powerless? How many, instead of directing the conversation with unbelievers toward spiritual matters, tend to stay in the 'safe zone'? Doing what Nellie did is a skill we need to develop and a challenge that comes straight from God. But we must look for these kind of openings. With sincere kindness and genuine concern we can turn almost any conversation to eternal matters – even if the subject is bee pollen! It's worth bearing in mind the following points when you're using your words to spread the *real* Word.

1 Keep it Short

A man attended a meeting where the guest lecturer was extremely long-winded. When the listener could not stand it any longer, he got up and slipped out of a side door. In the corridor he met a friend who asked, 'Has he finished yet?' 'Yes,' the man replied, 'he finished a long time ago, but he simply doesn't realize. He just won't stop!'

Coming straight to the point is excellent counsel for us as we talk with others each day. If we are honest with ourselves, much of our conversation is nothing more than empty talk. Jesus warned, 'For every idle word men may speak, they will give account of it in the day of judgement' (Matthew 12:36). Better to think carefully about what you say and listen more to what is spoken to you, than say too much without thinking at all about what you're saying!

2 Check Your Tone

Many years ago, a speech research unit at Kenyon College conducted a test in co-operation with the US Navy. The purpose was to discover how the tone quality of the voice affected sailors when they were given orders. A number of experiments revealed that the way a person was addressed determined to a large extent the kind of response he would make.

For example, when an individual was spoken to in a soft voice, he would answer in a similar manner. But when he was shouted at, his reply came back in the same sharp tone. This was true whether the communication was given face-to-face, or by telephone. So bear in mind those wise words from Proverbs: 'A soft answer turns away wrath' (15:1).

3 'Christ Has No Hands But Ours'

Jesus is in Heaven, but we are in view. We, as Christians, are Jesus' representatives here on earth; always ready, in the words of St Teresa of Avila, to 'go about doing good'. Our actions, behaviour and words are what draw people to pack halls, rugby stadiums and churches all over the country, often queuing up for hours to get into services. We have to show Heaven's splendour to the world, so our day-to-day ministry of simple Christian witness is vital.

4 Pray Constantly

The Lord can enable you to speak words that build up others and don't just fill the air. Today, make these words of David your prayer: 'Set a guard, O Lord, over my mouth; keep watch over the door of my lips' (Psalm 141:3).

THE TRANSFORMING POWER OF GOD'S WORD

I like to think of God's Word in this way: first, we read and study it; second, we act upon it; third – and, perhaps, most importantly – we share it.

Study God's Word with determination. It's not always easy: sometimes we find out things that we don't agree with; often, we may even have to 'unlearn' certain ideas that have been put across to us. Don't try to get around certain things or explain them away. Don't try to read things into the Word just because you want to believe things in a certain way. Accept the Word just as it is written.

Find out what God says in His Word about your place in His plan of redemption, what He means to you, what Jesus is doing for you right now and what the Holy Spirit is doing in you. Take your refuge in the Word of God, memorize it, let it get deep in your thinking – soon you'll discover that negativity begins to vanish, your confidence grows and a whole new perspective arises in you. You'll start learning about Jesus and getting to know Him personally.

Once you have come to know Jesus through the Word of God, you are ready to begin acting upon God's Word. After a while, acting upon God's Word becomes totally natural to you. It's then that you are able to share it with others, as this verse shows:

> After I've eaten, Lord,
> And on your word have fed,
> Help me share with others from
> Your precious, living bread.

Before we can serve the bread of life to others, we must feast on it ourselves. Similarly, as messengers of God, we must fill our hearts and minds with the truths of Scripture. Only then can we honestly give the Word's nourishing encouragement and exhortation to help others. The Lord told the prophet Ezekiel to eat a scroll that contained a message full of 'lamentations and mourning and woe' (Ezekiel 2:10). Because he was submissive to the Lord and applied the lesson to his own heart first, he could boldly present the life-giving message to all who would listen.

BELIEVE THE WORD

It's at our lowest times that we need to start believing the Word and speaking the Word as never before. The winds of time, adversity, Satan, trials, bad health, financial ruin: all these can beat on our door, on our minds, our lives. But who stands? Those who have heard the Word, the sayings of God, those who remember them and act upon them. The God we serve is an unlimited God. The secret is to remain steadfast and unaffected by this world's perversions. 'If evil come upon thee ... we stand before this house, and in thy presence ... and cry unto thee in our affliction, then thou wilt hear and help' (2 Chronicles 2:9).

Many are not anchored by His Word, they are like the man in the field, facing a mad, charging, angry bull. He jumps into a deep hole in the middle of the field only to discover there is a bear down there! So he has to leap back out to face the snorting, fierce bull and, as a result, isn't safe anywhere. As I've seen thousands of times, what's necessary is to get out of this 'down at heel' mentality and start praying for yourself, get others to pray for you, then go and serve someone else. Be a messenger of God, tell someone about Christ, and gradually you will feel a change deep within yourself. Without His Word we face either the bull or the bear, *with* His Word we can defeat both!

> *Whosoever heareth these sayings, remember*
> *them, hear them, hide them in your hearts ... and*
> *doeth them. I will liken him to a wise man who*
> *builds his house upon the rock, and when the*
> *winds beat on that house, it fell not.*
> MATTHEW 7:24–25

I'll sum up by focusing on these meaningful words: 'For the Word of God is quick and powerful, and sharper than any two-edged sword, piercing even to the dividing asunder of soul and spirit, and of the joints and marrow, and is a discerner of the thoughts and intents of the heart' (Hebrews 4:12). Believe in God's Word, act upon it, share it – you too will soon find yourself witnessing its all-transforming power!

- It's the Word in our minds – God's divine Word.
- It's the Word in our hearts – God's divine Truth.
- It's the Word on our tongue and lips – God's holy Book.
- It's the Word leading, inspiring us, giving triumph to us – God's precious commands and promises!

6

LONGING FOR GOD

'Blessed are you who are hungry now, for
you will be filled.'

LUKE 6:21

Between 1915 and 1950, an Australian nursing sister,
Elizabeth Kenny, devised a recuperation and healing
programme for people with polio. She was shunned by
doctors, turned down by medical boards, attacked by
the press, refused grants and money – even a Royal
Commission reported against her work. Yet thousands
recovered from this killer disease through her labours
and faith. At the end of her life her methods were
universally accepted and called 'The Kenny Way'. A
lone woman fought the whole establishment because
she was not satisfied with what medicine was doing for
these crippled people. She had a hunger, a curiosity to
find the answer, and she went a long way to discovering
a cure.

Curiosity is our in-built teacher that constantly challenges the status quo. It means that we become increas-
ingly determined to find out more, indeed, it can impel
us to search and hunger for truth, or knowledge.

Take this example. All over the world people use
aeroplanes. From huge airliners to small two-seaters,
aircraft have made the world into a neighbourhood.
Few people realize, however, that it all began in a

preacher's home. On returning home from a preaching trip, Bishop Milton Wright threw a small toy from his cupped hands into the air and to the delight of his two sons, Wilbur and Orville, a little elastic powered 'helicopter' flew across the room. This small action aroused an interest in flight that was to stay with the boys for the rest of their lives. Later, from their little bicycle shop in Dayton, Ohio, the Wright brothers began their long search for the secret of controlled, sustained flight. One evening, Wilbur was selling a bicycle tube to one of his customers and, as he chatted, he started unconsciously to twist the tube's pasteboard box in opposite directions in both his hands. When the customer had gone, Wilbur suddenly thought: 'Why did that pasteboard box not crack when I twisted it in opposite directions?' This simple question was to trigger a whole series of experiments, which would eventually lead to the development of flaps on a plane's wings, that are still successfully used today. The next time you go on holiday, and have to travel by plane, think of the Wright brothers, and the fact that your flight is being controlled by means of flaps on the plane's wings – flaps that have their origin in Wilbur Wright's bicycle tube box!

Curiosity has led to many other incredible inventions: it led Edison to the lightbulb; James Watt to the steam engine, Dunlop to rubber tyres, McAdam to tar, James Chalmers to the postage stamp, Bell to the telephone, Baird to the television, Einstein to his theory of relativity – even Rubic to his cube! All these people began with a desire to understand or find out something, and their hunger for knowledge was to lead to great things.

Our hunger for spiritual knowledge can be just as rewarding, if not more so. God loves to see in us a desire for Himself, a longing after Him, a taste for the best – a real spiritual appetite.

Smith Wigglesworth used to say, 'I'd rather have a man on my platform who had not received baptism in the Holy Spirit, who had no power, but was longing, hungry, dissatisfied and desperate for the blessing of the Lord, than a man who said he had received the fullness of the Spirit, and was quite satisfied and content and settled down.'

Remember Zaccheus? He was the swindler who was suddenly curious about Jesus, and so shinned up a tree to get a closer look. His curiosity led to Jesus inviting himself for dinner, and for Zaccheus to realize the error of his ways. His new-found spiritual hunger actually led him to repay many times over those he had cheated.

STREAMS IN THE DESERT

Often, it is in the times of most hardship that our hunger for God is at its strongest. The psalms are full of man's spiritual longing for God. In Psalm 63, King David is in the wilderness of Judah. He is fleeing from Absolom, who is attempting to steal his throne. Away from his palace and his normal comforts, facing rebellion in his family and loss of face in the nation, he cries out: 'Oh God, you are my God, earnestly I seek you; my soul thirsts for you, my body longs for you, in a dry and weary land where there is no water' (verse 1). C. H. Spurgeon says,

> *David did not leave off singing because he was in*
> *the wilderness, neither did he in slovenly idleness*
> *go on repeating psalms intended for other*
> *occasions; but he carefully made his worship*
> *suitable to his circumstances, and presented to*
> *his God a wilderness hymn when he was in the*
> *wilderness. There was no desert in his heart,*
> *though there was a desert around him.*

David is not seeking creature comforts nor the blood of his enemies, but in the windy, wild, wilderness is earnestly seeking his God. His physical needs and the desire of his soul are calling out in unison. Spurgeon continues:

> *A weary place and a weary heart make the*
> *presence of God the more desirable; if there be*
> *nothing below and nothing within to cheer, it is a*
> *thousand mercies that we may look up and find*
> *all we need.*

Other biblical stories of hope actually coming forth from the wilderness include those of Hagar, Moses and Elijah. Hagar (Genesis 16) was a slave girl, running away from Sarai, who was treating her cruelly. The angel of the Lord found her near a spring in the desert and comforted her, encouraging her to return and face the situation. She obeyed God's call and as a result of this experience of God in the wilderness, described Him as 'the God who sees'.

Exodus 3 describes how Moses saw God in the wilderness. It was while Moses was looking after his father-in-law's flock in the desert that God appeared to him in flames of fire from within a bush. In 1 Kings 17, we hear how Elijah was terribly afraid, actually running for his life. He journeyed into the desert, came to a broom tree, sat down under it and prayed that he might die. It was there that the Lord appeared to him, not in the earthquake or the fire but in a 'still, small voice'.

All these people are managing to reach out to God, despite being in the wilderness. It's almost as if they're saying to God, 'Lead on, my God, I'll follow as near as I can. I'll pursue you step by step, day by day and be as close to you as I possibly can.'

We, too, can often find ourselves in the wilderness. A sudden occurrence has made us feel that we are travelling through a desert of sorrow, or physical or mental suffering. We feel lost and forsaken by God. Everything seems arid and cheerless. It's in instances like these that we need to remind ourselves of those – like David, Moses and Elijah – who have discovered that God can and does make the wilderness blossom and 'streams in the desert' (Isaiah 35:6).

Think of John Bunyan, the preacher who spent 12 years in Bedford jail, because preaching the Gospel was unlawful for an unordained man. Bunyan lost his freedom and suffered bitter persecution, but out of that dark time came one of the world's most famous books, *The Pilgrim's Progress*. It opens with these words:

As I walked through the wilderness of this world,
I lighted on a certain place that was a den [his
prison] ...

Perhaps you know the story of Josephine Butler. When she returned home one evening from a meeting, her little daughter, hastening to greet her, fell over the landing-rail and lay dead at her mother's feet. Instead of shutting herself away in her agony of grief, Josephine Butler caused her wilderness to blossom, dedicating the rest of her life to caring for the despised 'girls of the street'. She became a mother to hundreds.

Mildred Cable, that intrepid missionary, travelled across the fearsome Gobi Desert with the Good News of the Gospel. Once, she and her companion retraced their steps to find a simple desert dweller to whom they had given the Gospel message. She was completely transformed. She had given up opium.

'She led us into a room,' said Miss Cable, 'On the wall was a picture we had given her of a flower opening up its petals to heaven though its roots were deep in the soil.'

'It is two years since you were here,' said the woman, 'and I have never smoked opium since. I could not go on displeasing God.' The desert had begun to bloom! 'The desert and the parched land will be glad; the wilderness will rejoice and blossom. Like the crocus, it will burst into bloom' (Isaiah 35:1).

'OUR RESTLESS SPIRITS YEARN FOR THEE'

A. W. Tozer said 'The impulse to pursue God originates with God, but the outworking of that impulse is our following hard after him.'

I have noticed over a number of years now that as my need for Him decreases so does my longing. But as my need increases, my longing accelerates both in desire and action. A. W. Tozer speaks clearly on this need for God:

> *I want to encourage this mighty longing after God. The lack of it has brought us to our present low estate. The stiff and wooden quality about our religious lives is a result of our lack of holy desire. Complacency is a deadly foe of all spiritual growth. Acute desire must be present or there will be no manifestation of Christ to His people. He waits to be wanted. Too bad with many of us He waits so long, so very long, in vain. If we would find God amid all the religious externals, we must first determine to find Him and then proceed in the way of simplicity.*

It *is* a many-splendoured thing to long after the living God. Don't lose your longing, don't treat it as common place or take it for granted. May our response always be like the psalmist: 'My heart says of you, "seek His face!" Your face, Lord I will seek' (Psalm 27:8).

This story elaborates further on our longing for God. It's about a child who became trapped in the attic of a burning house. One man in the crowd below held out his arms and shouted to the child to drop from the window. But the child remained where he was. At the last minute the boy's father came upon the scene. Opening his arms, he called, 'Jump, Robert, jump!' Without hesitation, the child jumped to safety. Longing for God is like this – it's a leap into the sure hands of God.

I read somewhere a legend of an angel who came one evening to the brink of a river and asked the boatman to ferry him across. When they reached the other shore, the angel rewarded the boatman with a handful of what appeared to be wooden shavings. In disgust the boatman threw them into the river. The next morning he found a few of the shavings still lying in his boat, and examining them more closely found they were shavings of pure gold. Longing for God is precious gold, so make sure you don't throw it away!

LONGING MEANS HARD WORK

The word 'work' is used hundreds of times in the Bible. Longing means to work at it. The only way we lose out in our search for God is by quitting, losing our desire. Believe in God's biggest dream and don't look back – after all, you can't drive forward by looking out of the rear window! Jesus warned, 'No man looking back, having put his hand to the plough, is fit for the Kingdom of God' (Luke 9:62). When God sees someone with longing, someone who will not quit, He looks down and says, 'There's someone I can use!'

During a recent hot summer, the long dry spell produced many parched fields – even the fells of Cumbria were no exception. One local farmer, however, seemed to have much greener grass than most. He had cleared out his silage just a little earlier than others had. Then, the day after cutting, he had spread slurry manure on the fields and during that night there had been a reasonable shower of rain. That was just about the last rain that he saw for many days. The result was that his fields had the best grass-growing conditions and maintained a deep green colour when everything was drying up and turning brown. At least one ewe and her two lambs realized that the grass was greener on the other side of the wall, as it were! Cumbrian dry-stone walls are meant to be sheep-proof. But nothing was going to stop this very determined sheep. She found a way out, over the top, and her two lambs followed. Soon they were enjoying the delicious, fresh grass. In the same way, God wants us to long and hunger after the rich green grass – the lovely spiritual blessings, the table spread with good things He has prepared for us. But it means climbing those walls and taking that high ground. Here's a good story to illustrate the point further.

A wealthy American was admiring the lawns of an Oxford College he was visiting.

'Say,' he said to the gardener, 'I'd love to have a lawn like this back home. Where do I start?'

'Well,' said the gardener thoughtfully, 'you'd first of all need some good English soil.'

'Oh, that's no problem,' said the American. 'I'll just have a few hundred tons shipped over.'

'You'll need grass seed,' said the gardener.

'That's fine,' came the reply.

'Then you must be certain that the ground's exactly level before you sow in the autumn, and the grass is cut and rolled in the spring. And, of course, it must be cut and rolled, and cut and rolled, and cut and rolled …'

'Okay,' said the American. 'How long exactly does this cutting and rolling go on?'

'Well,' said the gardener chuckling, 'if you want a lawn like this one, I should say about two hundred years!'

There are certainly no shortcuts to anything worthwhile.

When Jesus came many did not recognize Him. A preacher tells how one evening he stood with a group of friends as a fireworks display was just about to begin. While he waited, he turned and saw behind him an exceptionally glorious sunset. Excited, he exclaimed, 'Look at that!' But no one looked – they were too engrossed in watching a man lighting a common squib.

God came to earth in Jesus in a particularly unspectacular way, and despite the beauty and perfection of His life, often passed unrecognized in the midst of people. Someone once said, 'Opportunity is missed by most people because it is dressed in overalls and looks like work.' Do we long for God, but fail to recognize Him in our daily lives? We must be daring in our search for our Maker – brave and bold in our hunger and longing for the Saviour. 'Even a turtle doesn't get ahead unless he sticks his neck out,' it is said. George Bernard Shaw wrote, 'I found that nine out of ten things I did were a failure – so I did ten times more work, searching, investigating *and was a success*!'

Many keep looking back at their yesterdays and failings, their lack of advance and depth, their lack of growth in God; so they get depressed and give up. But you don't have to consume your tomorrows feeding your yesterdays! Shake off the shackles of the past and long only for your God. The past is past – it has no life! 'Brethren, I conclude myself not to have apprehended, but to press on towards the mark' (Philipians 3:13, 14). It is my hope that such curiosity will lead all us hungry seekers into the labyrinth of truth, refusing to stop until we have found it; for after all, the truth shall set us free. The truth, that is, as it is found in Jesus.

I'll end this chapter with these beautiful words, written in the twelfth century, that encapsulate our longing for God perfectly:

Jesus, thou Joy of loving hearts,
    Thou Fount of life, Thou light of men,
From the best bliss that earth imparts
    We turn unfilled to thee again.

Thy truth unchanged hath ever stood;
    Thou savest those that on thee call;
To them that seek thee thou art good,
    To them that find thee, all in all.

We taste thee, O thou living Bread,
    And long to feast upon thee still;
We drink of thee, the Fountain-head,
    And thirst our souls from thee to fill.

Our restless spirits yearn for thee,
    Where'er our changeful lot is cast, –
Glad when thy gracious smile we see,
    Blest when our faith can hold thee fast.

7

BE STILL FOR THE PRESENCE
OF THE LORD

For God alone my soul waits in silence;
from him comes my salvation.

PSALM 62:1

In all the hustle and bustle of daily life, it's easy to forget
to take time out and be alone with God. Among the
great thinkers of history who have testified to the vital
importance of contemplation and quietness before God
are Augustine, Brother Lawrence, George Fox, Thomas
Merton, David Brainerd and Evan Roberts. Dietrich
Bonhoeffer spoke of 'spiritual stillness'.

No matter where I am, or what time it is, I make a
point each day of setting time aside specifically to be
quiet, to be still with God. When I go before Him, I
keep my body still. At other times, I walk around the
room. I also read Scripture. In quietness I can concentrate my wandering mind. Control of the mind – the
emotions, the will and the intellect – is vital to the
miraculous ministry. Be still and listen. William James
wrote: 'It's important to cultivate your silence power
as it is your words or tongue.' In the words of
Isaiah 30:15, 'In quietness and confidence shall be
your strength'.

Jesus 'waxed strong in spirit', Scripture records. He
waited on His Father. He went aside and rested a while.

Isaiah reminds us: 'They that wait on the Lord, shall have new powers.' Wait in quietness. My team knows that just before a service, I must have absolute stillness and quiet. This enables me to live in the realm of the miracles. I teach my converts, my family, my close team members, my staff: Wait on God! Wait quietly on God! Waiting like this in stillness will bring satisfaction, peace, answers, power beyond compare! A badge I saw on a teenager I saw at the end of one of my great rallies in Melbourne, Australia, read 'Beware, I'm dangerous ... I've been waiting on God'.

Dr Wilbur Chapman was once in a room with the famous Praying Hyde. Hyde came in and turned the key, locked the door, got on his knees, never said a thing for five minutes. But Chapman said, 'Oh the Holy Presence, just to kneel with him in silence, one could feel God, near ...'

Pause a while in the midst of the 'millennial workaholics'. Turn aside from the chaffing pressure, the mad scrambling and panting feverishness we experience daily in our lives. Stop. Rest. Let your soul catch up with you. Give time to think things through with God. Job said, 'When He giveth quietness, who then can make trouble?' (Job 34:29). Elihu said 'Stand still and consider the wondrous works of God' (Job 37:14). Isaiah said 'Take heed and be quiet' (Isaiah 7:4). Sit in God's presence. Let Him flood your heart. Mary sat at the Master's feet, and with all that criticism going on around her, Jesus said: 'She has chosen the better part. And it will not be taken from her.'

That famous hymn advises:

> Take from our souls the strain and stress,
> And let our ordered lives confess,
> The beauty of Thy peace.

A SENSE OF THE NUMINOUS

In Acts 4:33 we read: 'With great power the apostles continued to testify to the Resurrection of the Lord Jesus'. A distinctive feature of the Early Church which made it such a spiritual force and power was this: it had a strong and pervading sense of the numinous. The word 'numinous' doesn't appear very much in evangelical writings, but it was a favourite word of men like C. S. Lewis, George Macdonald, and Rudolph Otto. The dictionary defines it as 'sensing the presence of divinity, awe-inspiring'. It is a word that describes the holy fear that we ought to experience when we wait quietly, and are aware that we are standing in the presence of the holy God.

When John the Apostle, banished to the island of Patmos, caught a vision of the glorified Christ, he 'fell at his feet as though dead' (Revelation 1:17). When Daniel realized he was in God's presence he said: 'I had no strength left, my face turned deathly pale' (Daniel 10:8). There can be no real knowledge of God unless there is a sense of the numinous.

What joy we feel when we experience this true holiness! Samuel Chadwick said: 'Holiness brings the soul into fellowship with the redeeming Son of God. When Believers rejoice in its possession, sinners are awakened and saved.' The truth of the great prayer of the writer of Hebrews needs to be experienced by us all:

> *Now the God of peace, that brought again from*
> *the dead our Lord Jesus, that great shepherd of*
> *the sheep, through the blood of the everlasting*
> *covenant, make you perfect in every good work*
> *to do His Will, working in you that which is*
> *well-pleasing in His sight, through Jesus Christ;*
> *to whom be glory forever and ever, Amen.*
>
> HEBREWS 13:20–21

YOU'LL NEVER WALK ALONE

By human effort alone we can make no difference to this anti-God, hostile society we live in. But what a difference we can make with a strong sense of God's presence. Jesus said, 'Without me you can do nothing.' But with His presence, we are winners all the way!

We can't keep this Good News to ourselves, though. We must go out with our Saviour, abiding in the miraculous – shaking cities, turning the tide of evil, winning multitudes to our Heavenly Father's love. Years ago, Harry Lomas kept a little village store in a remote part of Cumberland. It was open six days a week, and often in the evenings he would carry groceries to people who were ill. Sunday was a busy day for Harry, too. At a time when public transport was almost non-existent on Sundays, he would tramp miles over the hills to conduct services as a lay-preacher. Asked why he added this extra activity to an already full and busy week, he replied, 'Because I can't eat my bread alone.'

Thank God we don't walk alone. With the strong presence of God we are champions. We are uplifters and inspirers. People soon see that with Jesus, life is a piece of cake!

WALK BOLDLY

Boldly, we stand towards Heaven, earth and man. James wrote, 'Come boldly by the blood of the everlasting covenant.' The blood has cleansed us and it justifies us. The blood hides us and washes us. It delivers us, so be bold in His blood, His power. The more crucified I am, the bolder I get.

In Ephesians, Paul speaks of Him 'in whom we have boldness'. Some say we need more faith in the Church, or that we need more power in the Church. But we have faith: 'To every man is given a measure of faith.' I never pray for more faith, for faith comes from the Word of God. I just read the Bible, or I listen to Bible tapes – just pure Scripture being read as I drive my car, as I work in the office, as I travel by aeroplane at 30,000 feet or by train at 120 miles per hour, as I ride on the back of the ox in Malaysia – the Word of God, day and night, night and day. It gives me boldness. As King Solomon said, 'The righteous are as bold as a lion.'

Paul urged: 'Come boldly to the throne of God.' He shook Europe with his preaching. He converted the city of Ephesus with his crusades. He healed everyone on the island of Malta. Chief of apostles, an outstanding intellectual, a giant of a church leader – yet he asks the Church to pray for him. What did he ask the Church to pray for? 'Pray that I may speak boldly the mystery of the Gospel.' He asked God that he may be bold. The enemies of the Church noticed, in the Acts of the

Apostles, 'the boldness of Peter and John, perceiving that they had been with Jesus'. If we are with Him, give Him plenty of room, He will make us bold. God is working for you. That name belongs to you: the name of Jesus. If your flesh cries out doubts to you, if your head tells you the opposite to your faith, if your mind plays tricks with you, if you are so down you want to quit – *don't*! Rise up in Him. Seek boldness. Let Jesus carry the burden. Remember, He is in you to carry the discouragement, the defeat, the worry. He is in you to change your situation. Go forth boldly with the Word of God.

Be bold: don't limit God; don't keep the shining, glorious presence to yourself; don't keep the Good News to yourself. Be still, wait upon the Lord, and be filled to overflowing with His presence!

8

SURVIVING IN THE SPIRIT

> May the God of hope fill you with all joy
> and peace in believing, so that you may
> abound in hope by the power of the Holy
> Spirit.
>
> ROMANS 15:13

A good friend of mine, George, owns a guest house. One morning, around the breakfast table, he was talking about fishing to one of the residents, Brian.

'I went fishing off Clevedon Pier yesterday, and didn't catch anything,' lamented Brian.

'But you won't catch anything there,' replied George. 'You want to go to Portishead off Battery Point and when you cast out you will be in deep water.'

'Yes,' replied Brian ruefully, 'I'll be in deep water all right [he was thinking about his wife], for two fishing trips in two days is a bit much!'

We are all in deep water today in our personal lives, what with work and all its stress, family demands and community living. People are caving in, breaking up – even collapsing completely. A minister, ten days before his wedding, finds his fiancée – quite out of character – arrested by the police for punching a shop assistant. His marriage is cancelled and his world crumbles. They seemed like the perfect couple. A successful young pastor rings me: his wife (who is normally quite fit) is suddenly dangerously ill in hospital, and his 33-year-old brother dies the same day in a motorbike accident. A fine, law-abiding, upright, good-hearted 20-year-old Christian is attacked by three young thugs. He fights back for his life and in the tussle one of the hooligans is badly hurt. The police arrive and arrest the innocent young man, and he is later brought to court (with no witnesses in his favour) and charged with assault.

These certainly are trying times for everyone. It takes a radical step to deal with the hindrances within ourselves, and to grasp the divine energy that is steadily, constantly available to us all. We must always strive to stay in the Spirit. For it's when we have the Holy Spirit working within us that we see such life changes. God simply wants to manifest Himself through us, and the work that's needed for that comes through the Spirit. It burns the dross out of us, it makes us more like Jesus.

This true story shows what a staggering transformation the Holy Spirit can make. It's about a man called Gary, who rented a flat in a big city in England. He made his money by buying and selling drugs. One day, his landlord called as usual to collect the monthly rent. Normally a dry, miserable sort of chap, Gary was somewhat surprised to find him bubbling, happy and talkative. It turned out that his wife, who for years had suffered with a bad spine, even having to wear a surgical jacket, had been down to some evangelist ('What on earth is that?' Gary pondered) somewhere down in the big theatre in the centre of the city.

The landlord could not stop talking. 'She came home absolutely fit,' he exclaimed excitedly. 'She says that today she's got no pain – she's not even worn her steel medical jacket for her spine. She's actually walking about. She's helping me in the office with a happy face – and I've not seen her do that for years! She's not grumbling, grousing or nagging me at all – it's marvellous! She came home from the meeting last night, and for the first time in donkey's years touched her toes with ease, without any pain, leapt on her toes and did a dance round the front room. It's so marvellous, I'm going to go to see this evangelist for myself tonight and see what it's all about!'

After continuing in this way for several more minutes, he eventually said goodbye to Gary and left – only to return five minutes later because he'd forgotten to pick up the rent! This is really strange, thought young Gary. He'd never seen the landlord go away without the rent, let alone anyone captured by religion! In a theatre, did he say? Miracles? Gary had never really believed in anything for himself, but this had to be worth having a look at – especially since it was free.

The next night Gary went along to the meeting. He found people queuing up on the main street to go into the theatre. Large posters advertised myself and the team for the 'Miracle Healing Services'. He'd never heard of anyone queuing up to go into a religious service before! It was packed with over 1,000 people but Gary managed to get a seat near the back. What he witnessed was unlike anything he'd seen before: worship, lively dancing (folk doing a 'jig' in church was something to watch indeed!), sheer happiness on hundreds of faces, an unbelievably joyous atmosphere – it was simply marvellous!

Gary heard me preach a simple message of faith. He had never thought about personal faith before, and was captivated. He felt the power of God touch his life as he heard the words of the Bible, and was changed on the spot. He was later counselled by an experienced Christian helper, but he said it was in his seat that God broke him, melted him, showed him his awful sins and redeemed him. He became a new creation.

A year later, I visited that city again and met up with Gary. Well-dressed, happy and eager, I soon learnt that he hadn't missed a single church service after that meeting; in fact, he was there as soon as the doors opened! He married the young lady he had been living with, she too was converted (they already had a little child) and now they worshipped as a family together. On the evening of that meeting, when he'd answered God's call to him, he returned home and flushed all the drugs he possessed down the toilet; he gave up drug-taking that very day. He had since found a good job.

As he spoke he clutched a New Testament which looked tattered and worn. He had been given it new by a local church a day or two after his amazing conversion. He had read it through twelve times and its message had penetrated his life, enabling him to get in harmony with God. In one year, faith arising from the Word and the Spirit had lifted him to become a great soul winner – he had since won many others to Christ. As he understood and believed the message of God, great faith-power had been unlocked. He had learnt to pray and to practise the life of Christ. He had discovered the importance of bridling his tongue, found the answer to stress, and had been lost in the wonder of awe, worship and praise. Telling me in more depth about the power of the Holy Spirit moving deep within him that evening, he simply said: 'I wasn't the same man again.'

After finishing his remarkable story, he thanked me for revealing the power of God to him. 'I discovered what life was all about that night,' he said. 'I came alive, and through the teaching of Jesus, and the power of the Spirit, I have found how to keep fully alive ever since.'

By allowing the Holy Spirit to fill our lives, we are letting everything about us be empowered in the right way. In the eighteenth century, a clergyman asked the famous actor David Garrick how he could draw such crowds to the theatres of the land when the churches stood empty. Garrick replied: 'It is because I recite fiction as if it were fact, and you recite fact as if it were fiction.' 'We are witnesses of these things, and so is the Holy Spirit,' said Peter (Acts 5:32). We need more than a cold recital of facts if our brothers and sisters are to be convinced that what we say is true; we need a powerful display of the reality of what we say. The presence of the Holy Spirit is that display.

KEEP ENERGIZED!

To keep the Spirit alive within us, we need deep reserves of energy and resources such as never before. Emerson said: 'Energy is the spice of life, it is the energetic who are really living.'

When we lack energy, we cave in, give up and slow down, eventually coming to a stop – our whole life may even be marred. We find that our energies are dissipated on the wrong roads, the wrong quests, the wrong aims and the wrong destinations. We are missing God's riches, God's gems. A jewel thief was cornered and arrested in a London Underground station recently. The police also picked up what they thought was the bag of missing gems. But it was a similar bag to that of the train driver, who, when he had finished his shift later on that day, discovered that instead of a packed lunch, his bag contained jewels worth about a million pounds! Miles away the chuffed and delighted police inspector was dumbfounded when confronted, not with the loot, but a flask of tea and three cheese and pickle sandwiches!

Today, many weary, exhausted souls are exchanging God's positive riches, diamonds and hoards of blessing – for what? 'Dry cheese and pickle portions' of worry, despair and burdens! A second-hand car salesman, at the end of his tether, said to his minister one day, 'I'm leaving my job, I'm worn out. It's impossible to be a Christian and be up to this job's demands.' The clergyman replied, 'I don't believe that.' He read an extract from the Book of Titus to the man: 'To the pure all things are pure, but to the defiled nothing is pure ... be sober, reverent, sound in faith and love, in patience ... showing yourself integrity, incorruptibility ... that you may adorn the doctrine of God our Saviour' (1:15; 2:1, 2, 10).

He showed him that here was a great place to show the glistening glory of Christ, here was the right setting for the jewels of Jesus to shine at their best. The greater the test, the deeper the strain – the mightier the energy imparted to match the challenge.

Quietly Does It!

We live at too intense a pace. We study, when we should be meditating. We work, when we should be waiting upon the Lord. We dash, we fret at delays, we fume at disappointments, we lash ourselves into a flurry of activity – and accomplish little.

We must get away from the noise, bustle and crowds which fragment our minds, and listen to God in stillness. 'A meek and quiet spirit ... is precious' (1 Peter 3:4). Rider Haggard's mother brought up seven sons, without ever raising her voice to them. She explained, 'With seven noisy sons in the house, shouting would not do a bit of good. I found a whisper was much more effective!'

Go into a quiet place, do not talk, keep your body still, and listen. Consider these famous words of W. H. Davies:

> What is this life, if full of care,
> We have no time to stand and stare.
> No time to stand beneath the boughs,
> And stare as long as sheep and cows.
>
> No time to see, when woods we pass,
> Where squirrels hide their nuts in grass.
> No time to see, in broad daylight,
> Streams full of stars like skies at night.
>
> No time to turn at Beauty's glance,
> And watch her feet, how they can dance.
> No time to wait till her mouth can,
> Enrich that smile her eyes began.

A poor life this if, full of care,
We have no time to stand and stare.

Silent moments are not pathetic escapism or delusions. They are creative, dynamic and confidence-boosting. In the silence, put your problem in the hand of God. Think of it being solved in God's way, which is the right way. Believe that the healing peace of God is touching your mind, that the blocks that have prevented anointing, power and victory from flowing through us are being removed, and let the answer float through to the top of your mind. How many times when tired and facing immense problems, and even somewhat tense, I have felt it all evaporate before me!

The words of this 'Twenty-third Psalm for Busy People' are most suitable!

The Lord is my pace-setter, I shall not rush.
He makes me stop and rest for quiet intervals.
He provides me with images of stillness
Which restore my serenity.
He leads me in the ways of effectiveness,
Through calmness of mind,
And His guidance is peace.
Even though I have a great many things to accomplish each day,
I will not fret, for His presence is here.
His timelessness, His all-importance, will keep me in balance.
He prepares refreshment and renewal in the midst of my activity,
By anointing my mind with His oils of tranquillity,

My cup of joyous energy overflows.
Surely harmony and effectiveness shall be the fruit of my hours,
For I shall walk at the pace of My Lord,
And dwell in His house forever.

It's when we use these moments of calm that we can effectively reflect on our life. I'm sure, like me, there'll be good times and bad times, but maybe you'll discover that you've been able to learn from past mistakes and actually turn failures into successes. John Newton, frustrated that he had not achieved all the success he had sought for, worn out, his energy low, began to muse on his journey in life and discovered he was not the failure he had previously presumed. After much quiet thought, he wrote: 'I am not what I ought to be, I'm not what I want to be, I'm not what I hoped to be, but thank God I'm not what I used to be!'

Don't Panic!

One of the gangsters in Quentin Tarantino's film *Reservoir Dogs* says '*the worst thing we can do is panic inside*'. Perhaps you are worn down by worry. Maybe you're stressed by responsibilities at home or work, or concerned about your health or future. The story is told of a farmer who raised chickens. Among them was a rooster whose occasional crowing annoyed the farmer's neighbour. Early one morning, this very disgruntled neighbour rang the farmer and complained. 'That awful bird of yours keeps me up all night.'

'Well, I can't understand that at all,' replied the farmer. 'The rooster hardly ever crows. Even if he does it's never more than two or three times.'

'Look, you don't understand,' retorted the neighbour. '*That* isn't my problem. It's not how often he crows that irritates me. What keeps me awake is not knowing when he might crow!'

How many of us are like that neighbour? We panic and worry about any difficulties and distressing circumstances that could arise tomorrow, rather than living each day at a time and rejoicing in the Lord's sufficiency for the present. Meditate on these words from Matthew's gospel: 'Do not worry about tomorrow, for tomorrow will worry about its own things' (6:34). Take time out, turn to Jesus, and receive from Him that stream of renewing power which can release you from your stress and give you peace. God really is on the scene. He feels as we do, weeps as we do, suffers as we do: what a wonderful counsellor!

'O Thou Lord of Life, Send My Roots Rain'

Haven't we all, at some time or another, cried out to God in this way? Gerard Manley Hopkins' words aptly convey our real need of help.

When you feel badly let down, the spirit drains, hurt wells up, energy vanishes, frustration increases. One of these times might be when you've felt betrayed – one of the toughest tests we can face while serving God. I saw it happen to a loving pastor. He encouraged a gifted teenager in his congregation to go to Bible school. He arranged for financial support, and continued to support the young man after graduation, letting him preach on occasions. But then the graduate began to undermine the pastor with innuendo and criticism. Finally the heartbroken minister left. Then the young man announced himself as a candidate for pastor of the church.

Jesus knows all about betrayal. He invested three years into the lives of His twelve disciples, for one of them – Judas – to betray Him for 30 pieces of silver. But Jesus isn't going anywhere – on the contrary, it's when we feel the most let down that He makes us firm. It's through our dilemmas that we are introduced to greater energies, and so stay in the Spirit; the attacks and adversities that we come up against can actually help deliver us into a place of abundant resources.

Look at the tenderness of the Last Supper, as Jesus sat in calmness around the table with His disciples. They ate, talked and relaxed, yet it was the prelude of arrest, denial and despair. We see Judas walking away, betrayal, Peter weeping, violence, suicide, political skulduggery: all this following such a tranquil scene. Finally, Jesus agonizingly dies on the cross. Truly, out of the worst of happenings such victory, such blessing, such a redemption, such a hope for all mankind can emerge.

Out of our dilemmas, therefore, we can gain the right attitude, by grasping the nettle, catching the wind with our sail of positive faith and understanding, by right thinking. A new wave of fresh empowerment and energy will help us to sustain healthy, happy living. Turn your impediments into stepping stones to a new future; have a will to win against all the odds!

LOOK UP AND SEE ONLY GOD

Paul said: 'I have learned the secret of being content in any and every situation, whether well fed or hungry, whether living in plenty or in want' (Philippians 4:12). We, too, no matter if the demands of life are easy or hard, comfortable or painful, secure or insecure, should not be dominated by them: we should see only God at all times. The secret that Paul is talking about is that Jesus is with us to give us the strength and resources to cope. As the Amplified Bible puts it: 'I have strength for all things in Christ who empowers me – I am ready for anything and equal to anything through Him who infuses inner strength into me, that is, I am self-sufficient in Christ's sufficiency.'

External factors in life may knock us down, but the Spirit of Jesus Christ, dwelling within us, ensures we are never knocked out. He is our source of constant survival, and our means of facing life at every turn with unshatterable confidence.

The 'secret' is an open secret. Its experience is the birthright of every Christian. Our only barrier is our pride and unwillingness to deny our sense of independence, and live in dependency on *God alone*. We preach and proclaim not a programme but a *person*; not a system, but a *saviour*; not a movement, but a *master*; not a creed, but a *Christ*. I like this beautiful meditation:

> Look up! Look up at the sky!
> Who created all those stars you see?
> The One who leads them out like an army.

He knows how many there are.
He calls each one by name.
His power is so great, not one is ever missing!

Look up at the sky!
Stop putting yourself at the centre of your world.
See the greatness of God
And you'll see everything in true perspective.

Look up at the sky!
Lift your heart above the synthetic
And glimpse One so much greater.
His glory is reflected in the changing sky,
His greatness and majesty are beyond compare!
He made the universe
And all that's in it.
His power can't be measured
Nor His glory imagined.
Look up at the sky!

A worldly reporter talked to me after a successful healing service, in one of the great cities of England. After seeing the blind see, cripples run, wheelchairs pushed away, crutches and sticks and canes and walking frames all carried away by happy relatives following the cure of their loved ones, he asked, 'What is this power? I'm amazed – what is its source?' I replied, 'This energy and power is from the wounds, the suffering, the crucifixion of Jesus.'

I know God is a loving, kind, good God. I have demonstrated that God answers prayer, heals the sick, works miracles, supplies my needs. I believe in what God has given me to do. I am a sincere hard worker, honest and have faith. I expect God to help me, and know when it is not immediate it will come sooner or later. God is the source that never fails. I will not limit God – ever!

LET THERE BE LIGHT

When they installed flood lighting in St James' Park, Newcastle United's football ground (a great novelty in those days), and the first two lights were switched on, there was a great roar of delight. As more and more lights went on, more applause reverberated around the ground; when they were all working, the ground was flooded with light.

As we open up more and more of our lives to Him, God gives us increased joy, energy and light. Our journey through life will get brighter and brighter as we let God's light illumine our way. 'I keep lifting the corner for you ... lifting the darkness, giving you more light and energy, revealing more inner strength, revealing more and more of Jesus until He is fully revealed' (1 Peter 4:13).

This verse came into my hands last week:

A little boy told me the other day
He always said a prayer to God at night.
'And in the morning, too?' I asked.
'Oh no,' said he, 'I'm not afraid when it is light.'
The childish answer lingered in my mind;
I wonder, do I seek God when I find
The darkness round me ... do I ask His aid
Only when I'm lonely and afraid?

I think that God must like to hear from us
When we're happy ... when our way is light;
He'll help us through our saddest, darkest hours
But let us seek Him too, when skies are bright.

So when you feel too weak, too small or too flattened to face up to life's demands, just remember these fantastic words of Betty Rees: 'If you think you are too small to be effective you have never been in bed with a mosquito!'

9

SUCCESS THROUGH FAILURE

'The God of heaven is the one who will give
us success ...'

NEHEMIAH 2:20

About seven years ago, a pastor made a comment about
my ministry which got back to me. 'He's had his day,
he's nearly finished, no one will want him in another six
months. His ministry will have flipped out shortly' was
the gist of it. It would have been easy to take those
words to heart and think that failure was on its way.
But the truth is that in these past seven years my
ministry has actually grown more rapidly than ever
before and reached more people; I have even seen more
miracles and travelled to more nations to preach the
Gospel!

It's easy, isn't it, to get discouraged and believe that
you are failing yourself, your family and friends and
Jesus. Perhaps you have drifted from the faith. Perhaps
a daughter or grandchild has gone wrong morally.
Perhaps a son is into drugs. Perhaps boredom, frustration and emptiness has come into your relationship
with your husband or wife.

A man I know, a loving pastor, was once told by
someone in his congregation, 'There's not a single word
you've said in the last few years that has meant
anything to me.' That finished him. He quit the pulpit,

and almost had a breakdown. He fell to the great temptation in failure – discouragement. Events persuaded him that he'd never get to where he wanted to go. This kind of situation is one we've all faced. In whatever guise failure appears, it will seem insurmountable and almost crippling. It will hit you like a wave, and it seems that nothing – even faith in God – will stop the force of the impact.

KEEP ON THE RIGHT TRACK

You may think failure is the opposite of success. If you aim for success in some aspect of your life, and miss it, then you've failed. You fail if you miss that promotion, fail if your engagement breaks off, fail if you give in to that temptation.

But beware! Failure tries to make us think it's the terminus, a place where the track stops, when in fact it's only a station along the line. Never think of failure as going the wrong way at a set of points and landing up in the wrong place. Instead, always think of it as a wayside stop, a place where you may have to linger for a while, but which lies on the route to your ultimate destination. Failure can be turned to good, stumbling stones become stepping stones of blessing, peace, glory, joy, victory and honour in your life.

The one fear to conquer is the fear of failure. After all, I'd rather attempt something great and fail than attempt nothing and succeed. I admire people who make a commitment and stick their neck out to achieve it. I admire a person who tries to reach the top and doesn't make it. Our failures, Samuel said, are 'as a

small thing in thy sight O Lord God' (2 Samuel 7:19).
Say with the Psalmist 'I beat them small as dust' (Psalm
22:43).

When we read some of the Psalms, we find ourselves
nodding in agreement to some of David's words. For
example:

> *I am the scorn of all my adversaries, a horror to*
> *my neighbours,*
> *An object of dread to my acquaintances; those*
> *who see me in the street flee from me.*
> *I have passed out of mind like one who is dead;*
> *I have become like a broken vessel ...*
> PSALM 31:11–12

But David didn't stop there. A few verses later we read
this marvellous affirmation of his faith in God:

> *But I trust in thee, O Lord, I say 'Thou art my*
> *God.'*
> *My times are in thy hand; deliver me from the*
> *hand of my enemies and persecutors ...*
> PSALM 31:14–15

Somehow David made that transition from failure to
success. He chose to stop pushing the car, as it were, and
to jump into the driving seat. He took one look along
the platform of failure and got straight back on to the
train. He refused to let himself be discouraged, refused
to take his eyes off his final destination, even when he
was deep in trouble. So what was David's secret? These
five 'don'ts' for failure may give you a clue!

1 Don't Be Hypnotized by Failure

Because failure's happening to us right now, it casts a sense of doom over everything we do. It feels as though we'll never be rid of it. But, in fact, every trouble goes in the end. We all talk about having 'a sense of perspective' and 'not seeing the wood for the trees'; we've all looked back on a problem and wondered why it caused us so much distress.

I was at Heathrow airport recently on a very cloudy morning, listening to my fellow passengers moan about the weather. There wasn't a happy face around! And yet as soon as the plane took off we rose through that thick pall of cloud to find ourselves flying in bright sunshine. Suddenly everybody began to smile and look cheerful. I thought to myself: 'That's a perfect example of how we are with God. The cloud of failure darkens our world because it cuts us off from the light.'

Norman Vincent Peale said: 'If you visualize failure, you tend to create the conditions that produce failure.' So what's important is not to look at it, but to look at God. Get the situation in perspective. Don't be like the lifelong pessimist whose only consolation was to write on his gravestone: 'I told you so!'

2 Don't Think You're the Only One

Two teardrops are floating side by side down a big river. One of them asks the other: 'Who are you?'

'I'm the teardrop from a girl who loved a man, but lost him to another,' is the reply. 'And who are you?'

'Ah,' says the first, 'I'm the teardrop from the girl who got him!'

Failure often produces a real sense of isolation in the sufferer, as though they're the only one to have ever felt this way. But we really aren't alone in our sufferings; the same things have been happening to Christians the world over for centuries. Think of Peter, the first apostle, who began his work with the dismal failure of denying the man to whom, just a few hours before, he'd serve to the point of death. Believe me, there is not a single successful person who has not at some time tasted the bitterness of failure. Oscar Wilde was thrown into prison. Winston Churchill was thrown out of office – right after he'd led Britain to victory in the Second World War. Daniel was thrown into the lions' den. But they all succeeded in the end!

3 Don't Think Failure Will Last Forever

Diamonds may last forever, but not failure. Life is so constructed that different experiences follow one another. If you have failed now, that doesn't mean you will feel the effect of it for the rest of your life. Tomorrow is another day: 'Weeping may tarry for the night, but joy comes with the morning' (Psalm 30:5). If Peter got over his failure, you can get over yours!

4 Don't Ignore the Potential in Failure

God doesn't allow failures to happen to us to make us miserable. He allows us the experience so that we may find in them the seeds of future success.

When David was fleeing Saul, the first place he went to was Gath. If he hoped to win friends there, however, he was mistaken – he was soon recognized as a commander of Saul's army and taken for interrogation by the king. He was saved from death by pretending he was mad, and left Gath as alone as he'd been when he arrived. Or, almost as alone – he next found himself in charge of an army of 400 men, but ragamuffins at that! He might well have considered his plight to be hopeless. And yet out of these unlikely beginnings God was building a force that would take David to the pinnacle of success – the throne of Israel. David made use of what God gave him. We need to do the same. As C. H. Spurgeon said: 'God gets His best soldiers out of the highlands of affliction.'

5 Don't Forget to Follow Through

It's all too easy when one failure is behind you to heave a sigh of relief and slacken off. Don't! If you don't learn from it, you'll soon be back there.

A few years ago, a young American called Bob Weiland walked across America. It took him two years to complete the journey. Describing his incredible feat, he said: 'Faith is never passive. When I started walking I didn't sit there thinking, "Okay, Lord, if you want me to cross America, take me." When I started I took a step, then another and another and here I am today, one thousand, six hundred miles down the road.' What's so extraordinary about that? Well, Bob did that walk on his hands – his legs were blown off by a mortar shell in Vietnam. What would you have done if you'd been crippled like that? Would you have given up?

DARE TO SUCCEED

To overcome failure involves daring and risk taking – are you up to the challenge?

Winston Churchill said in his book about painting that when one approaches the easel with palette and brush, the canvas seems to look up and say 'You dare!' Oscar Wilde declared that 'an idea that is not daring is hardly worth calling on'. No daring – no wisdom gained. Seize opportunities, take advantage of them. There's never a shortage of new things to learn and people to help. As Teddy Roosevelt said, 'Far better to dare mighty things, even though checkered by some failures, than rank with those poor spirits who enjoy neither victory nor defeat.' You see, even if someone loses the battle, he is still a winner, because he has conquered his fear by trying. In doing so, he has won his biggest battle. Every loser who tries to do something great is really a winner.

Through risking we:

- uncover great opportunities
- discover beautiful solutions
- overcome impossible obstacles
- unwrap surprises God has in store
- roll back the dark clouds until the sunlight breaks through.

By daring you see:

- a goal you should be pursuing
- a dream you should be launching
- a plan you should be executing
- a project you should be starting
- a possibility you should be exploring
- an opportunity you should be grabbing
- an idea you should be working
- a problem you should be tackling
- a decision you should be making.

John F. Kennedy said: 'If you have taken one step on a thousand-mile journey, you are a step nearer your destination.'

A mistake we often make is to look at the thousand miles and decide the first step isn't worth taking. When commencing any task there is an inertia to be overcome, and the drive to succeed is no exception. But remember that God gives us strength. If we stay rooted on the ground we won't get anywhere. But once we begin, one step at a time will see us over an enormous distance. Jump in, risk, dare for God. Yes, jump at every opportunity, every chance and every door God opens in front of you. As a school boy I was often reprimanded for jumping in at the deep end, but I'm not sure it's such a bad habit to get into. My son Paul served in the British Paratroop Regiment for a while – he jumped from planes! – and always maintained that 'courage comes when you dare, when you try, when you jump!'

LIGHT FROM DARKNESS

David and Jackie Hendry, from Glenrothes, were devastated when their longed-for baby died only three days after she was born. They kept asking themselves, 'why us?' Jackie was often reduced to tears by well-meaning folk who told her she was young and would have other children.

As the days dragged on, they tried to come to terms with their grief by keeping themselves busy. They decided to spend a couple of weeks hill walking. Pausing by the edge of a waterfall, fascinated by the mass of water pouring into the depths below, Jackie suddenly spotted a tiny, wild cherry tree clinging to a narrow ledge, its white blossoms soaked by the spray from the torrent. In this dark and perilous place, apparently in constant danger, the tree had rooted itself and put out the flowers which promised fruit later in the year. It was like a message for them both, saying that the dark days of winter don't last forever.

Jackie and David returned from their holiday feeling more at peace than at any time since their tragedy. They've a long way to go yet, but the memory of the cherry tree is always with them. They can at last look forward to happier times ahead.

Even though you may feel a failure in practical ways, remember that failure does not necessarily mean the end in terms of spiritual experience. There are no scrap heaps of discarded Christians. As we bring our failure, hurt and bad experiences to God and give them over to Him, we discover He is the God of redemption. He is able to make all things operate for our good. He will act in forgiveness towards our repentance. He builds strength into those areas of weakness we have confessed and admitted.

Jackie and David's story shows that we can move from despair and failure to hope and a bright future; from deep darkness to light, sunshine and hope. The very act of Jesus' death and resurrection says the same.

10

FAITH THAT MOVES MOUNTAINS

Above all, taking the shield of faith,
wherewith ye shall be able to quench all the
fiery darts of the wicked.

EPHESIANS 6:16

A lady was visiting some friends one evening. After a very pleasant time spent chatting and laughing, she decided she ought to be getting home. She was about to leave when she saw her friends' son in the garden. The boy was holding a ball of string.

'What are you doing,' said the lady curiously.

'Flying my kite,' he replied.

She looked up but could see only the stars twinkling in the night sky.

'How do you know your kite is up there?' she queried.

'It's easy,' said the boy, 'I can feel it tugging at the string.'

Faith is like that. We can't see God, yet we know He is there. We feel His presence. We have the tug of the string of faith, which ties us to Him.

The unbeliever challenged the Christian: 'How can you believe in something you cannot see?'

The Christian replied: 'Ever had a headache?'

The man nodded. 'Oh yes, many times.'

'Did you see the headache?'

The sceptic looked quizzical. 'No, never.'

'How do you know then that you have it?'

The unbeliever, getting a bit nervous now, replied: 'Well, I felt it.'

The Christian rejoiced and said, 'Exactly, I feel God, every moment. Each day, He is with me.'

YOKED TO CHRIST

The greatest power in the whole world, so I believe, is the power of faith. Chadwick said, 'Without faith man can do nothing with God, and God can do nothing with man.' Faith holds firm in storm and calm, peace and despair, joy and sorrow. We need faith through the good times, as well as the bad. On a recent television interview, the presenter turned to me and said – with a somewhat cynical air – 'All this faith business is a leap into the dark!' 'Oh no, sir,' I replied with a smile, 'it is a *leap into the light*!'

My family and I once went to the stunning island of Sark, off Jersey. No cars are permitted on the island, but they do have taxis of a sort – horses and carts! Most of the island tours were beyond my price range, but at the very end of the line was an elderly driver with an elderly horse, and he offered to 'do a deal'.

We climbed aboard the rickety old cart, which rattled and shook as we set off on our grand tour. Some while later, the driver passed the reins to my son, who was only young. I was worried, to say the least. We were going past cliff tops – what if we rolled over? What if my son made the horse take a wrong turn? To my surprise, however, my son managed very well: when he pulled right we turned right, and when he pulled left we turned left. The blinkered horse had no idea where he was headed; he simply obeyed. He trusted the driver implicitly. We all have a lesson to learn from that. Jesus said, 'Take my yoke and put it on you, and learn from me, because I am gentle and humble in spirit; and you will find rest. For the yoke I will give you is easy, and the load I will put on you is light.'

To be yoked to Christ means what it says. We are blinkered, and He steers. We don't know the road ahead, but He does. We are servants, but He is the Master. As we actively seek His guidance for our lives, we discover what it means to be disciples. We can't expect to plan our own lives in the Lord's service, nor choose the opportunities we think are best. We must actively seek the Lord's will and submit ourselves to it – even when we don't agree! The key to success is to find the lock, and that lock is faith and submission to God. Faith must be built on holiness and obedience, resulting in personal victory, a spiritually sweet disposition, love, joy and peace, and a right relationship and kind attitude to others. These are as much the mark of men and women of biblical faith as receiving all the things we need and desire.

FAITH FACTS

These words of F. F. Bosworth, however, are most telling: 'Most Christians feed their bodies three hot meals a day, but their souls one cold meal a week, and they wonder why they are so weak in faith.' That is, we have to work at it as well! We have to keep our side of the bargain. How do we do this?

Some Christians say to me, 'I just don't have any faith. I've prayed and fasted for faith, but I just don't have any.' Asking for faith will never produce faith. Why not? Because faith doesn't come by asking, 'faith comes by *hearing*, and hearing the Word of God' (Romans 10:17).

Having to encourage Christians to develop their faith means that the Word of God has lost its reality in their lives. None of the New Testament Epistles encourage believers to have faith. Why not? Because the Epistles were written to the Church, and its individual members – as now – were actually born into the family of God. Believers have received the Holy Spirit as their teacher, guide, and comforter. And the measure of their faith will be the measure of their knowledge of their Father – and their knowledge of their privileges. And that will be the measure of your faith too. Simply study the Bible and get acquainted with your heavenly Father. Walk in the closest possible fellowship with Him. Become familiar with your privileges as His child. As you become one with the Word, and the Word becomes one with you, you will become mighty in faith.

Keep persevering! In the words of St Paul to Timothy: 'Finish the course, keep the faith' (2 Timothy 4:7). A little sparrow was perched on the edge of a bird bath in a park. Some women strolling through the park stopped to watch him. 'What's the matter with the poor little thing?' one asked. Another commented, 'Let me pick him up and take him home and give him some warmth, he seems ill.'

Just then, another lady who had been watching nearby stepped in. 'Leave him alone, don't destroy his self-confidence,' she said. 'He's just getting a start in life, that's all.'

The ladies stood in silence, watching the sparrow as it gradually built up the courage to fly a few feet. Soon, he was surrounded by other birds, as if they were encouraging him as well. It wasn't long before he was flying up off the birdbath into the air with all the other birds flying alongside him. The ladies watching marvelled at his spirit, perseverance and final confidence. So our faith involves dedication and perseverance. Reject all that blocks the flow of faith. We fail when we are not willing enough to practise the power of faith. We fail to unlock our faith power.

Not that it's easy, mind you! Sometimes we feel that we lack faith or that the faith we once had is weakening. Throughout our faith journey, we should always ask for God's help and support – we can't do it all ourselves! The headmaster of a fine Christian school in London, for example, spoke recently about how this splendid school was brought into being from unpromising beginnings. He reflected how the banks had their doubts – at times they almost wrote the school off. But he had faith in God. 'I believe in God's law of supply and demand,' he said, 'and that He never fails. I just kept on believing this big task had to be done and that faith in the Father would bring this work through.'

Take John Wesley, that inspirational, marvellous preacher. On his first missionary journey to America, he found himself unsure and anxious that he didn't know God personally. On the ship he met some godly Moravian Brethren – dedicated missionary Christians, zealous, full of loving and faith. He noted that when storms and winds surrounded the boat, nearly causing it to sink, these Brethren had no fear but rather sang Psalms and were filled at all times with infectious joy and calm. He felt impelled to talk with them about his own fear, and so explained to one of the leaders that he simply couldn't grasp personal faith. The leader's reply was to burn in his heart and lodge in his spirit, even strengthening him for over 50 years of evangelization in the British Isles. 'Have such a faith,' the leader responded, 'but if you don't, then *say* you have such a faith until it takes hold of you!' As it says in Romans, 'Faith is the evidence of things not seen', and again 'I call things that be not, as though they were'.

What about this testimony? My friend, a minister, told me about a situation of disappointment that had practically destroyed his faith, but how – in the end – it led to ultimate triumph through Christ. The particular project he was working on at Westminster Central Hall had been rejected by a committee assessing it. Eighteen months of work had been rejected by a vote of 13–9, with no right of appeal. Hurdle upon hurdle had been faced and surmounted, but now it seemed as if it were all a waste. My friend was deeply disappointed. On his way home by train, he gazed out of the window, mentally replaying the brief encounter in the committee room, wondering if he should have said or done something different. It was only when he was in church, kneeling at the communion table, that he suddenly realized that what really mattered was knowing and having faith in God. 'I looked up at the bread and wine and remembered again what love He had for me ... We may not understand the disappointments and confusions of our lives, but when we wear the yoke of obedience we know that He will guide.'

WALKING BY FAITH OR BY SIGHT?

Many Christians want to live by faith, but at the same time they want *to walk by sight*. In other words, they want to know God's entire plan for their lives before they will even take *one* step of faith or obedience. That's not walking by faith – that's walking by sight. By trying to guess what God has in store for you, by trying to see further down the road than God wants to show you, you'll end up in a mess – more than likely taking others with you.

When you walk by faith, you've sometimes got to take just one step at a time. Determine in your heart to live by the Word of God and to never quit or turn back. By doing this, you'll look back and see just how far you've come. That's how you will walk *by faith* over any mountain or across any valley, through any trouble or around any adverse circumstance. One step of faith and obedience can bring you into the joy of the Lord and the fulfilment of the promise of God in your life.

FAITH GROWS STRONGER AS WE CLIMB HIGHER

Few experiences match the challenge and exhilaration of mountain climbing. Those who participate in this exercise of endurance and skill like to compare peaks and share experiences. When European climbers get together to swap stories, they often tell of passing a certain grave along the trail to a famous peak. On the marker is a man's name and this inscription: HE DIED CLIMBING.

To me, mountain climbing is a picture of the life of faith. Throughout our lives we are to continue moving upward – learning more about God, growing in our relationship with Christ. The author of Hebrews put it this way: 'Let us run with endurance.' The words with endurance may be translated 'with perseverance'. Joshua was just such a man of God. His 'climb' began in Egypt and ended in the Promised Land. He won great battles. We are told that 'Israel served the LORD all the days of Joshua' (Joshua 24:31) At the close of his life, Joshua was still urging Israel to serve God faithfully (v. 23). Like Joshua, let us run with endurance the race that is set before us.

As we grow in faith, we'll find God's blessing pouring out even further. As Dr W. Sangster put it: 'Faith is like the sluice gates on a canal or river. You move the great wheel and the gates move a little, and a small trickle of water seeps through. Turn the wheel full course and the flood gates open to their widest and you have a flood of power and blessing.' In Christ we are kings, and by faith the powers of heaven are unlocked to us. There is no limit to what God can do for those who practise his laws of faith.

When you buy a new car, you receive a warranty which assures its quality for a few years. This is the guarantee from the car manufacturer that it will stand by its product. If something happens, the company has to stand by its guarantee and give you the necessary support to get the problem solved. With God, the guarantee is *limitless*, it is complete, the full warranty will always be honoured! 'You keep your promises to those who try to do your will' (1 Kings 8:23); 'If thou canst believe, all things are possible' (Matthew 9:23); these awe-inspiring Scripture passages are so appropriate. Christ never fails, He is the author of our faith. Don't doubt, but rather submit gladly, give yourself, all you have, fill yourself with the fullness of God until you can no longer take anymore.

Faith sees the invisible, believes the incredible, and receives the impossible, as the old saying goes. It means believing what God says solely because He said it to us. Abraham and Isaac all started out on God's naked Word, risked all on God's Word, submitted to the fact that what He said he would do, He *did* do. Believing in Him is to stake everything, your very life, on the fact He is true to His words. Dr Martin Lloyd Jones said believing is 'to take the bare word and act upon it'. The urgent, glorious, eternal, transforming Gospel is applicable, every bit of it, for today.

OAKS FROM ACORNS

Trusting in God and having faith in what He wants for us isn't easy, especially when what He's offering us is literally life changing! Wesley was settled down in a nice curacy, but God shook him up to ride out and save England. Carey mended boots in his Northampton cobbler's shop, but God spoke to him and sent him to India. Jackie Pullinger was rejected by the official missionary societies, but she still went and has since made an enormous contribution to Christian missionary work in Hong Kong.

David Livingstone (1813–73) could have had an easy life as a doctor in Scotland, but God breathed on him, and so Africa was opened to Christ. David Livingstone knelt down and prayed, surrendering himself to Christ's will. He resolved: 'I will place no value on anything I have or possess unless it is in relationship to the Kingdom of God.' In his last journals wrote: 'We punted six hours to a little islet, a pitiless pelting rain came on, the wind tore the text out of our hands, the loads are all soaked – but nothing earthly will make me give up my work in despair. I encourage myself in the Lord, my God.' The inscription over his burial place in Westminster Abbey reads, 'For thirty years his life was spent in the unwearied effort to evangelize.'

A young man went west some years ago and found himself in California with no more than a few dollars in his pocket. He went to a bank, and said to the manager: 'I want to buy a garage. Will you lend me some money?'

'I'm sorry,' said the manager, 'if you've no security behind you we can't do anything for you.'

The door was slammed in the young man's face. What did he do? What would you have done? Given up? Well, he got a job at the smallest garage in Los Angeles. He worked hard. In five years, what had been the smallest became the biggest garage thereabouts. Then he went back to see the bank manager, and got an advance of $150,000. Today, he's behind one of the biggest motor services in the United States.

See the idea? One door shuts, but another opens – accept the challenge! Start like a little seed, bury yourself in God, and by His hand it will grow into a mighty work and blessing for Him.

On your faith journey, if you feel for whatever reason that your faith has weakened and that you need support and comfort, these words should help in your time of need:

> *The simple truth is that if you had a mere kernel*
> *of faith, a poppy seed, say, you would tell this*
> *mountain – 'Move!', and it would move, and*
> *there is nothing you wouldn't be able to tackle!*
> MATTHEW 17:20–21, TRANSLATED
> BY EUGENE H. PETERSON IN
> *The Message*

– 11 –

FAITH BY EXAMPLE

Fight the good fight of faith; take hold of
the eternal life, to which you were called …
1 TIMOTHY 6:12

The Bible introduces to us many characters who have experienced the power of faith. As we read their life stories, we can see that these weren't necessarily *great* men and women, but they were men and women who had *great faith*. When confronted with impossibilities, they didn't just give up – they each made a far-reaching decision and held on tenaciously to their faith in God! Their decisions ultimately meant their triumph of faith was recorded for us in the Word of God, to use as an example for ever. By looking at the challenges they faced, we are helped to surmount the difficulties we face, the trying circumstances which sometimes seem to cry at us 'You can't make it! You're going to fail! There's no way you can do what God has told you to do!'

What's vital is that we understand that they overcame obstacles by putting their faith in God, not simply because they had faith in their own abilities. They knew God would help them through every trial into what He had promised them. These godly men and women of the Bible realized they could not get the best God had for them if they quit believing and trusting Him.

From the very first pages of Genesis to the last pages of the Book of Revelation, God gives His people the same loving, timeless message: 'Don't give up! Keep on trusting me! I will make you victorious in life!' God in His mercy has interwoven this message throughout the Word of God because He desires to encourage and inspire mankind, knowing His creation will face challenging obstacles in life from time to time. And because of the challenges and opposition we do sometimes face in life, there's probably not one person who has ever lived upon this earth who hasn't at one time or another thought, what's the use! I might just as well give up!

However, we must realize that sometimes even the great patriarchs of the Bible – from Abraham, the father of many nations, to John, the Apostle, who penned the Book of Revelation on the Isle of Patmos – were faced with many of the same questions, perplexities and trials we've faced in our own generation. In the face of sometimes insurmountable difficulties, godly men and women in the Bible had to make the same decision Christians today must make: Should I quit? Should I just give up and forget what God has promised me? Can I really believe that what God has promised, He is able also to perform?

DANIEL

Daniel, a Hebrew who was probably of royal descent, was a man full of surprises and faith. He had great courage and stood up for what he believed in. For example, he adamantly refused to go against Jewish Law and eat the King's meal – as he had been requested to do by the King – as it would violate his Hebraic training and godly upbringing. He knew that by disobeying the Law he would be displeasing God, and that he couldn't bear!

> And the king [Nebuchadnezzar] appointed them a daily provision of the king's meat, and the wine which he drank; ... that at the end thereof they might stand before the king. But Daniel purposed in his heart that he would not defile himself with the portion of the king's meat, nor with the wine which he drank: therefore he requested ... that he might not defile himself.
>
> DANIEL 1:5, 8

What were the results of such resolve? Well, Daniel was given 'understanding in all visions and dreams' by God (1:17). When Daniel came before the King, he was found to be 'ten times better than all the magicians and astrologers that were in all his realm' (1:20).

However, circumstances got rough once again when Daniel came up against further laws and pressures imposed which were contrary to his commitment to God. A proclamation went forth that no one was to seek counsel of any man – or God – for thirty days. If anyone did, it meant instant death. The person who defied the King's command would be thrown alive into a den of hungry lions!

How many of us have faced a lions' den because of our faith in God? That would be a test of our faith, wouldn't it? Let's examine Daniel's faith in the midst of a circumstance which would probably daunt the faith of even the most courageous!

Even though Daniel remained faithful to God, he still had to face the lions' den. That's important for us to see, because sometimes we think that when we walk with God there will be no tests or trials in life. We may not have to face a lions' den in our lives, but there *will* be trials that test our faith. Daniel's faith did not waver as he faced the lions. And his faith in God did not go unrewarded because God sent an angel to shut the mouths of those hungry lions. But the key to Daniel's success and triumph over the evil plan of the enemy is found in verse 22:

> *My God hath sent his angel, and hath shut the lions' mouths, that they have not hurt me: forasmuch as before him innocence was found in me; and also before thee, O king, have I done no hurt.*

In other words, Daniel was innocent before God and man. So, although evil men rose up against Daniel and tried to destroy him, God protected him because Daniel walked uprightly before God *and* man. Daniel was found blameless in his ways before God; therefore, no evil scheme could prosper against him! Not only that, because Daniel's ways pleased God, even though Daniel had to face this trial, God promoted him so that he became one of the most important men in the entire Babylonian Empire.

What is important for us to see in this passage of Scripture is that regardless of circumstances, because Daniel purposed in his heart to please God, he put himself *in a position* to receive from God.

BARTIMAEUS

Another account in the Bible shows us a man who would not give up his faith in God, even in the face of insurmountable obstacles – blind Bartimaeus. We can envisage Bartimaeus on the Jericho road clutching his rags and shivering in the cold as he sits begging by the side of the road.

> *And when he heard that it was Jesus of Nazareth, he began to cry out, and say, Jesus, thou son of David, have mercy on me ... And Jesus stood still, and commanded him to be called. And they called the blind man, saying unto him, Be of good comfort, rise; he calleth thee. And he, casting away his garment, rose, and came to Jesus. And Jesus answered and said unto him, what wilt thou that I should do unto thee? The blind man said unto him, Lord, that I might receive my sight. And Jesus said unto him, Go thy way; thy faith hath made thee whole. And immediately he received his sight, and followed Jesus in the way.*
>
> MARK 10:47, 49–52

Let's picture this scene from Jesus' viewpoint. As He walked down that dusty Jericho road, He heard a desperate cry. He stopped in His tracks when He heard that piercing cry of faith! There was something in that cry – it was a voice of such strong faith and conviction in God's power that it insisted upon being heard. It was a voice filled with faith that would not quit and refused to be silenced. Seeing is not believing because Bartimaeus was blind and could not see!

Bartimaeus' strong faith could not be denied, silenced or refused. That's the kind of faith that will cause blind eyes to be opened! Bartimaeus was convinced that Jesus could heal him. He was totally convinced of God's power working on his behalf, and that is faith. He refused to be denied his chance of God's best for his life. Bartimaeus realized he had to seize the moment; this was *his* hour, and he had to take his healing with a violent kind of faith which would not be denied.

Do you have that kind of faith which refuses to take no for an answer? It's time you begin to cry out to God with a voice of faith that won't be denied! The cry of faith *will not* be silenced and it *cannot* be quenched. The cry of real faith will never quit or give up!

RISKING IT ALL

Let's look at the obstacles that stood between Bartimaeus and his prayer being answered. For one thing, in the crowd that met Jesus as He travelled along the Jericho road, I'm sure there were many cold, starchy 'religious' people of the day. Because religion adheres strictly to man's traditions instead of embracing an active faith in Jesus, the religious zealots of the day probably could not endure the sound of faith as it came from the lips of Bartimaeus. Religion tries to subdue and altogether extinguish faith, and if there were religious zealots in this crowd, they were probably the very ones who kept telling Bartimaeus, 'Hold your peace!' (Mark 10:48).

Religion can be a great obstacle and hindrance to faith, but Bartimaeus determined that *no obstacle* was going to keep him from receiving what he wanted from God! Religion or no religion – no one was going to make Bartimaeus be quiet and lose out on his blessing from God! – he dared, he insisted, he believed!

Bartimaeus was a risker. Faith that wins is one that takes risks. I like the lines of Phil Happa:

> To laugh is to risk appearing the fool,
> To weep is to risk appearing sentimental.
> To reach for another is to risk involvement.
> To expose your feelings is to risk exposing your true self.
> To place your ideas, your dreams, before a crowd is to risk their loss.
> To love is to risk not being loved in return.
> To love is to risk dying.
> To believe is to risk despair.
> To try is to risk failure.
> But risks must be taken, because the greatest hazard in life is to risk nothing.
> The people who risk nothing, do nothing, have nothing, are nothing.
> They may avoid suffering and sorrow, but they cannot learn, feel, change, grow, love, live.
> Chained by their attitudes they are slaves; they have forfeited their freedom.
> Only a person who risks is free.

Bartimaeus received what he wanted from God because he didn't compromise his faith in God. Let's be sure none of us compromise our faith and settle for less than God's best for our own lives. I don't know about you, but I want to receive the very best God has to offer! I will never compromise! I will go on to victory, and so will you, so take God at His Word!

UNITE IN FAITH

And straightaway many were gathered together, insomuch that there was no room to receive them, no, not so much as about the door: and he preached the word unto them. And they came unto him, bringing one sick of the palsy ... And when they could not come nigh unto him for the press, they uncovered the roof where he was: and when they had broken it up, they let down the bed wherein the sick of the palsy lay. When Jesus saw their faith, he said unto the sick of the palsy, Son, thy sins be forgiven thee.

MARK 2:2–5

The power of God was available to heal every single person in that house, but only *one* man was healed, and he wasn't even in the house! Why was he healed when no one else was? Well, because his companions persisted in their task in spite of a major obstacle, and were united in their purpose to see their friend healed. In other words, they were united in faith.

That man on the stretcher and the four who carried him could have given up when they saw the crowd of people closed in around the door of the house where Jesus was preaching the Word. They could have said, 'Well, we might as well go home, this is impossible. Let's not even try.' And that sick man would have been carried back home just as sick as he ever was. But they didn't give up; they persisted in their faith. Also, when they couldn't get into the house, they could have said something we often hear people in our day and age say, 'Well, I guess it just wasn't the Lord's will after all.' That's the way a lot of people determine the Lord's will – by circumstance. But the Lord's will is not determined by the circumstances we face in life. God's will is already declared and set forth in His Word, and it includes healing!

I imagine it was fairly easy to take the tiles off the roof of that particular type of house. But, on the other hand, I suspect it must have been a little unnerving for those who were in the house listening to Jesus preach and teach the Word, and all of a sudden hearing the tiles of the roof being pulled off! Can you imagine how the man who *owned* the house felt as those four men were tearing up his roof?

But the important point is that when these five men were confronted with an obstacle, they didn't give up; they did something about it! When they couldn't get to Jesus, their faith wasn't deterred – they just went around another way. The Bible says that God will always provide a way of escape. It took some faith to move that obstacle – to climb up on that roof and to lower that sick man down into the house. And it took some faith on the part of the man who was sick with palsy too: not only was he already bedfast, but one false step as his friends were carrying him up to the roof, and he could have been worse off than he was before!

To do anything for God corporately we have to be in unity – unity of purpose, unity of goal and unity of action. For example, the Acts of the Apostles continually talk about the apostles being in unity or in one accord. Every time the disciples were in unity, the power of God was in such manifestation that in one place it says the very house where they prayed was shaken (Acts 4:31).

CALM, PERSISTENT FAITH

A friend who's a veterinary surgeon told me this story. He was phoned after midnight by the owner of a labrador puppy. The dog had been stung by a bee. The agitated owner described how his dog wouldn't settle and kept licking the sore spot. After making sure there was no swelling or trouble with the dog's breathing, my friend told him to bathe the sting in a solution of bicarbonate of soda and warm water.

'Is that all?' the owner asked anxiously. 'What about aspirin?'

The vet considered for a moment.

'All right,' he said. 'You'd better take two – it'll will help calm you down.'

Keep calm in your faith! Some Christians are trying to walk by faith, but they have no commitment and don't keep a cool head, so when the slightest trial comes up, they say, 'Well, we'll *try* this faith business, but if it doesn't work, we can always try something else.' By staying calm, knowing that God will be there for us, we can manage what looks impossible, and so keep our faith alive. The Bible says it's your *faith* that pleases God. But how can your faith please God if you're always wanting to give up in the trials of life! There's no backbone to that kind of faith!

You see, persistent faith is tenacious. It doesn't let go of the desired goal no matter what Satan may try to throw in its way, and no matter what obstacles may have to be overcome; persistent faith keeps on believing God regardless of circumstances. Persistent faith fights the good fight of faith.

Strong faith and strong commitment are 'buddies'. To use an illustration – you can't shake hands with someone unless you have someone else's hand to shake. But if two people shake hands in agreement about something, they come into one accord on that issue. In the same way, when strong faith on the one hand comes into agreement with strong commitment on the other hand – that creates the kind of faith that will get something done on the earth to God's glory! That creates the same kind of explosive force for God as the natural and the supernatural coming together – it makes an explosive force for God!

SURRENDER IN FAITH

No matter how faithful we have been, even if we have been used to tremendous, outstanding miraculous results and great anointing, God has still *more* to give us than ever before. Junk does build up in our lives, so He wants to give us even better things. He wants greater fruit, tenderness, openness to unusual leadings and obedience – all so that we are literally ready for anything. Pin this list up somewhere where you can see it every day and see how your faith grows through surrendering to God.

- Surrender your spirit to Christ for fulfilment.
- Surrender your body to Christ for dominion.
- Surrender your will to Christ for occupation.
- Surrender your mind to Christ for mastery.
- Surrender your conscience to Christ for control.
- Surrender your mobility to Christ for purity.
- Surrender your talents to Christ for leadership.
- Surrender your relationships to Christ for His glory.
- Surrender your destiny to Christ for eternal life.

If ever you feel that your commitment is weak and your faith diminishing, remember that faith keeps the sails of life filled with the breath of heaven. True faith is not just believing that God can, it is knowing that He *will*.

> At times our fears may loom so large,
> We long for proof that God is near;
> It's then our Father says to us,
> Have faith, my child, and do not fear.

SERVING GOD, SERVING OTHERS

> Like good stewards of the manifold grace of
> God, serve one another with whatever gift
> each of you has received.
>
> 1 PETER 4:10

Perhaps one of the most effective advertisements ever written appeared in a London newspaper earlier in this century. It read: 'Men wanted for hazardous journey. Small wages, bitter cold, long months of complete darkness, constant danger. Safe return doubtful.' The advertisement was placed by Sir Ernest Shackleton (1874–1922), the famous Antartic explorer. Commenting on the overwhelming response he received, Shackleton said, 'It seemed as though all the men in Great Britain were determined to accompany us.' They were evidently men of great courage, willing to undergo extreme sacrifice for a worthy cause.

Shackleton's advertisement reminds me of the words of Christ: 'If anyone desires to come after Me, let him deny himself, and take up his cross, and follow Me' (Matthew 16:24). Jesus was also looking for those who would go with Him on a hazardous journey – the way of the cross. This call was issued by the Lord after He had indicated to His disciples that He was going to Jerusalem to suffer and be killed. Thousands have responded to that invitation down through the centuries, gladly forsaking all to follow Him. But are we hindered in our attempt to follow Jesus?

When Julius Caesar landed in Britain with his Roman legions, he took an incisive, bold step to ensure the success of his military venture. He ordered his men to march to the edge of the cliffs of Dover, and commanded them to look down. To their astonishment, they saw every one of their ships engulfed in flames. All forms of retreat had been deliberately cut off. There was nothing the soldiers could do but advance and conquer – which they did.

A similar psychology for our discipleship is suggested by Jesus. All His followers must break all ties that weaken or interfere with wholehearted commitment to Him:

> ... *whoever of you does not forsake all that he has cannot be My disciple.*
>
> LUKE 14:33

No person or thing should ever come before Him, as he meant when he said that we had to renounce all material possessions, and put Jesus above all – even above our families. Here's the all-important question: is any earthly attachment hindering our allegiance to Christ? If there is, maybe we need to 'burn some boats'.

WHATSOEVER YOU DO, TO THE LEAST OF MY BROTHERS ...

You may think it's an awesome task to give up everything and follow Jesus, and so it is. But we can all begin in small ways. Perhaps one of the easiest is to show our love for Jesus by loving those around us, helping them in their hour of need. I want to appeal to you to be a POW, a 'person on watch'. Keep alert to people under pressure, be a support and encouragement to them.

One experience I still hold very vividly in my memory is that of the death of my father. He was marvellous, and very sadly died at the age of 52 from cancer. The whole family was devastated. Some Christians came to us with appropriate Bible verses and others came with what I feel was nothing more than religious clichés. I have no doubt that the people concerned were very well meaning but they certainly did not minister to my need at the time. But there was one man, however, who came to visit me and yet never said a word – his tears simply mingled with mine. Words cannot express what that meant to me. F. W. Robertson commented: 'One act of love will teach us more of the love of God than a thousand sermons.' You can preach a sermon without saying a word.

Someone wrote: 'A man all wrapped up in himself makes a very small parcel indeed.' I have come across some very small parcels, even in Christian circles. At times we can get so locked into our own personal situations, which maybe are quite small, that we fail to see people around us struggling with mountainous circumstances.

I have a motto on my office notice board that is a constant challenge: 'Great occasions for serving God come seldom, but little ones surround us daily.' Some Christians look for the great opportunities to be involved in Christian service and yet miss the obvious.

Every year Amnesty International appeals for people to send Christmas cards to them, which will then be sent to people all round the world who are in prison for their beliefs. Margaret Forrester, an Edinburgh minister, put her name and address on the card she sent in, and weeks later a letter came back from the man who'd received it, a Protestant pastor in a jail in Indonesia.

Margaret couldn't make head nor tail of it. It was a jumble of numbers and letters. The only words she could make out were a mixture of letters and numbers, like Phil 414, Gala134 and Matt2536, for example. They made no sense until she realized they stood for Philippians 4:14, Galatians 1:3–4 and Matthew 25:36 and so on.

As she looked up each text in her Bible and wrote it down, to her amazement a letter appeared. It read: 'It was kind of you to share the burden of my troubles. I thank God whenever I think of you, and when I pray for you all, my prayers are always joyful. When I was ill, you came to my help, and when in prison you visited me. May God bless you all the days of your life, and may you live to see your children's children. Let us never tire of doing good, for if we keep going, we shall in due time reap our harvest. God is with us!'

She realized that the Indonesian prisoner, unable to write in English, had used his knowledge of the Bible to send her a courageous message which bridged all barriers of language, censorship and distance, thanking her and assuring her that he was in good heart.

That Sunday, as Margaret told her congregation the story of the letter and read it out, she could not hold back her tears, and there was scarcely a dry eye in the church. Here was a persecuted believer who climbed his mountain, who found a way through – spurred on, no doubt, by that small act of kindness that Margaret had carried out.

Did you hear about those children in Edinburgh who took fizzy drink cans to church on Easter Sunday? All through Lent they denied themselves these fizzy drinks, and used the money saved to help homeless children in South Africa. To supply a bed and bedding in one of the hostels being set up for hundreds of street children in Cape Town costs £30. The total amount the children raised came to almost £500, much of it in copper, along with some cheques. It's amazing what can be done with some cans, thoughts for others and a bit of self-sacrifice!

PARTICIPATE!

A church without a minister expressed to me their concern and desire to appoint one. They commented: 'We need someone who will go out and get the people in!' I made the point that church growth is not dependent upon a spiritual superman but is the responsibility of every member: 'The body grows and builds itself up in love as each part does its work' (Ephesians 4:16).

The Bible very clearly teaches us that every Christian is expected to be a partner in participation. Every believer is called into membership (Romans 12:5) and ligamentship (Ephesians 4:16). The very practical teaching of 1 Corinthians 12 and Romans 12 is that every member of the body of Christ is important and each has a vital contribution to make. What appear to

be the insignificant parts of the body are actually essential: 'On the contrary, those parts of the body that seem
to be weaker are indispensable' (1 Corinthians 12:22).
And what a variety and multiplicity of gifts are
mentioned: helping others, the gifts of administration,
encouraging, contributing to the needs of others, hospitality – to name but a few. John Oxenhand wrote some
lines that are called 'What can a little chap do?' which
show how we can live our lives in service for others:

> What can a little chap do
> For his country and for you?
> What can a little chap do?
> He can play a straight game all through;
> That's one good thing he can do.

> He can fight like a knight,
> For the Truth and the Right;
> That's another good thing he can do.

> He can shun all that's mean,
> He can keep himself clean,
> Both without and within;
> That's a very fine thing he can do.

> His soul he can brace,
> Against everything base,
> And the trace will be seen,
> All his life in his face;
> That's an excellent thing he can do.

> He can look to the light,
> He can keep his thought white,
> He can fight the great fight,

He can do with his might,
What is good in God's sight;
Those are truly great things he can do.

Though his years be but few,
If he keeps himself true,
He can march in the queue,
Of the Good and the Great,
Who battled with Fate,
And won through;
That's a wonderful thing he can do.

And – in each little thing,
He can follow the King,
Yes – in each smallest thing
He can follow the King
He can follow the Christ, the King.

– 13 –

FINDING THE EXTRAORDINARY
IN THE ORDINARY

You are my lamp, O Lord; The Lord turns
my darkness into light. With your help I can
advance against a troop, with my God I can
scale a wall.

2 SAMUEL 22:29

A well-known English preacher was booked to speak at
a week-long Bible course held in a Butlin's holiday
camp. He, along with many other eminent preachers,
was the main speaker at the big rallies held every
evening. All these preachers had many years' experience between them and were immensely practised in
their art.

And yet, it wasn't *any* of them that made the most
impact on the crowds that night. It was a man called
Fred, who shared the testimony of his dramatic conversion in Dartmoor high security prison where he was
serving a long sentence for several crimes. His down-to-
earth words and heartfelt cries of thanks and praise to
God were miraculous; little did he think, even just a few
months' back, that he'd be in that situation, witnessing
to so many people.

The Apostle Paul was considered by many to be just
plain ordinary. Some critics wrote about him: 'His
letters are weighty and forceful, but in person he is

unimpressive and his speaking amounts to nothing' (2 Corinthians 10:10). But who was a greater purveyor of the treasures of eternity than Paul? He travelled hundreds of miles in wild country, among even wilder men, to carry the unsearchable riches of Christ and at what cost to himself? He gladly endured cold, hunger, stonings and imprisonments so that he might share God's Word with others. His letters still encourage, guide, inspire and cleanse millions today!

Extraordinary? Me?

What's even more amazing is that God wants each and every one of us – no matter how ordinary we may feel. I was an apprentice bricklayer in Wiltshire when the Lord called me to His service. Even in that ordinary setting of work amongst the bricks, I felt I was able to serve God by talking to my colleagues, doing extra jobs, answering their many questions about my beliefs. Some are still good friends now! God assured me that he'd use me where I was – and He did!

My work began on a small scale, preaching in local churches, city halls, chapels and at small groups throughout England. Gradually, however, my ministry grew to where I was spending many weeks away from home, in all parts of world, preaching the saving power of God's Word. One week I could be in the Thai-Malay jungle bringing Christ to hundreds of local people, another I could be establishing a new church in another country, or appearing on television or in the newspapers.

My healing ministry also grew in strength, and our crusades saw blind people regaining their sight, cripples walking, little children saved from death, asthmatics cleared of all their respiratory problems and people with cancer miraculously seeing their tumours disappear, for example. Media interest also developed in intensity, and I was able to reach so many more people by crusades held in football and rugby grounds. Throughout all this, God has always been faithful to my calling. He has protected me through thick and thin. Therefore, I have always repaid Him by spreading the Gospel and thousands have been born again.

Through the dark 1950s, the permissive 1960s, the violent 1970s, the upheavals and rapid changes of the 1980s, and now into the moral decay and desperate 1990s to the end of a century and the doorway to a new millennium, God has blessed me, an ordinary bricklayer from Wiltshire, by honouring the ministry He gave me so long ago.

ONE GREATER THAN THE TEMPLE IS HERE

The Temple in Jerusalem at the time of Christ was a magnificent building. It took 46 years to build and immense skill and huge financial resources were lavished upon it. It covered an area of about 10 acres and employed 7,200 priests and 9,600 Levites who were on duty according to a well-arranged rota system.

There was a large supporting staff of bakers, barbers, weavers, incense-makers, treasurers, masons, carpenters, door- and gate-keepers, a doctor and many others, all of whom helped to keep the ritual of the Temple running, according to Jewish tradition.

The Temple symbolized the commitment of God to His people. The permanence of the Temple, its massive stones and careful design, demonstrated that God's concern for Israel was permanent. He was not going to move on somewhere else, and His people were not expected to move either. The Temple was permanent because God is permanent and the giving of the Temple showed God's pledge to His people. And yet, *Jesus said that He was greater than the Temple*.

Jesus said, 'One greater than Solomon is here' (Matthew 12:42). He has all authority in heaven and upon earth. Zechariah said he would 'change the land in one day' (Zechariah 3:9). He is on the scene, He will sweep away the Brussels bureaucrats and the Westminster Parliament. He will close down the White House and take over the Bundesbank, the London Stock Exchange, the Tokyo Stock Market and Wall Street, all in one day! And 'the kingdom of the world [will] become the kingdom of our Lord and of His Christ, and He will reign for ever and ever'.

Your ministry may be in a totally different sphere to mine, but the miraculous, almighty power of Jesus can be experienced just the same, no matter how difficult or impossible it may seem to us. Not once has God ever said, 'I'm sorry, Heaven is out of that blessing; we don't have any more', 'I'm sorry, you'll have to settle for less than the best' or 'I'm sorry, I can't do that for you because I don't know how'! God's ears are always open to hear the cry of the righteous (Psalm 34:15). Because Jesus purchased our total redemption on the cross, there is no problem that is unsolvable and there is no fear that is unconquerable. Your needs may be pressing, but your uncompromised faith in God will see you through to victory! All the onslaughts of hell and all the forces of evil combined cannot vanquish the power of a steadfast, uncompromising faith in God.

Are you facing insurmountable odds? Are you groping for your way as if in a dark tunnel? Are you saying 'I can't possibly do this?' Whatever you feel or think, God can help you. He is able to turn whatever seems humanly difficult or impossible into that which is gloriously possible. He is able to do immeasurably more than we ask or think.

FINDING THE EXTRAORDINARY THROUGH PRAYER

A little girl was coming home from school one wet and windy night. Just as she crossed the grass verge outside her house, the lid of her little case flew open, and out fell her school books and things. Hurriedly she picked them up and ran indoors. But when she got in she discovered her pencil sharpener was missing. 'And it was such a nice sharpener,' she said tearfully.

The next morning she rose early and ran out to have another look for her treasure. Bless me, if she didn't come running in with it a few seconds later! 'I suddenly remembered I hadn't prayed about it,' she said to her mother. 'So I told God, and asked Him to look with me, and He did – and so I found it!'

A little lad was watching what gardeners call a 'prayer plant'. 'Why is it called that?' he asked. I explained that it closes up in the evening and opens again in the morning – just as we do with our prayers.

After thinking about this for a while, he suggested, 'I'll stay up all night and listen to it!' May we all stay up and listen to God – maybe that way we'll hear what He's trying to tell us.

I remember the time I preached in a tiny village in the heart of Ireland, a staunchly Roman Catholic community that had not experienced a healing crusade before. A small group of ladies invited me to be the pioneer of such a crusade – little did they know that they were going to witness real revival! But before I had started the service on the first night, God warned me of some impending trouble. As Paul had said: 'An angel appeared to me this night in a dream. The ship will be lost but not one occupant on board will die.' My message was quite similar!

Opposition to my crusade grew: my posters were all torn down; the Civic Hall I had hired came under some heavy stoning; glass was thrown at us. The Garda (police) had to be called, who arrived quickly and were heavily armed.

However, just when it was probably thought least likely, God moved amongst us. At one of our healing services, a little blind child began to experience an improvement in his sight. Soon I had the favour of hundreds of people, and they flocked to the public hall, ignoring all efforts to persuade them otherwise. Mighty, awesome healings and miracles were worked in the glorious grace and name of our Saviour. He was glorified. The village was stirred by revival fire.

A gracious presence came down. The strong presence and the outstanding salvation wonders achieved revealed to us that we were close to a real revival. On that occasion in Ireland, as on many others, the Almighty was saying to me: 'Don't be afraid. Let me show you how much power is at my disposal!' How did God answer the people's prayers in that small Irish village? As a result of their prayers. As obedient people, having life in the Spirit, sharing in unity and fellowship with the living God, they went forward boldly to receive Jesus afresh into their lives and so saw marvellous events take place.

God wants us to jump deep into the waters. So many of us have the spiritual equivalent of 'hydrophobia'. We are afraid of getting into the water. But we must not be content only to paddle, or complain that the water is either too warm or too cold for our liking. Our summons is not merely to stay in the shallows but to be immersed, to be baptized, to be filled with God's Spirit. God comes near to us by the power of His Holy Spirit: beginning with the Church, He mounts in our lives a shop-front window display of what His Kingdom is like and, by that, advertises what He can do for those still outside, if they will only enter in. The challenge for all of us is to get more than our feet wet in the river of God's Spirit; it is for us to 'take the plunge' and enter into all that God intends for His Kingdom. With prayer, we too can gain the fortitude necessary to go deep into the Kingdom of God. As Sherlock Holmes said to his assistant, 'These are deep waters indeed, Watson.'

– 14 –

MOVING IN THE MIRACULOUS

> 'I have no silver or gold, but what I have I
> give you [the paralysed man]; in the name
> of Jesus Christ of Nazareth, stand up and
> walk.' And he took him by the right hand
> and raised him up.
>
> ACTS 3:6–7

We have lived through 'the day of small things' as the Prophet said in the Old Testament. Isaiah also wrote of his time: 'The inhabitants were of small power' (37:27). God wants you to have *great* power, to do the impossible, to achieve the incredible. He desires for us to move in the miraculous power of the Holy Spirit, working with Him in blessing, delivering, saving and healing mankind. You may not be a preacher, vicar, pastor or evangelist, but you can move mountains, pray power down and work miracles. As you can see from the list below, which is only a very small sample, Scripture is full of references to the gift of the Spirit we can receive.

- The manifestation of the Spirit is given to every person (1 Corinthians 12:7)
- Your Heavenly Father knows how to give good gifts. (Matthew 7:11)
- See that ye come behind in no gift. (1 Corinthians 1:7)

- Come to the full measure of the gift of Christ. (Ephesians 4:7)
- Neglect not the gift. (1 Timothy 4:14)
- Stir up the gift that is in thee. (2 Timothy 1:6)
- There are diversities of gifts. (1 Corinthians 12:4)

So, how do we work miracles? Is there a key? Does it work for everybody? How can anyone get to say what the missionary Hudson Taylor said: 'First it's impossible, secondly it's difficult, thirdly it's done!'? The key, I believe, is keeping hold of God's power within us. Sometimes, although we taste the power and strength of God, we can actually lose the taste for it. In practical terms, we must hold fast to God's purpose, we must persist, commit ourselves fully and pay attention to the smallest detail. These are among the keys to manifesting the real excitement of God's miracle-working.

FULL SUBMISSION

We begin by remembering that we can all do more with our lives than we are doing at the moment; that is, we are all called to more than we are doing at present. When we are called, we must submit. There is no point in God calling us to do something if we do not listen to Him. And there is no point in listening if we do not do as He asks: that is what full submission means. Garibaldi, the great nineteenth-century Italian leader, stood before thousands of his fellow countrymen and called to them: 'I offer you no wages, no home, no food. I only offer you thirst, hunger, forced marches, battle, bloodshed, perhaps even death. But let him who loves his country with all his heart – follow me!' And they did! Tens of thousands sacrificed their daily comforts and desires so that together they might grasp a greater glory.

The ten points I outline below are a good basis to start you thinking how you, too, can move in the miraculous with God; and in the next chapter, I outline how you can stay in that blessing.

1 Desire to Be Used

We strive, strain and toil, get all heated up and get weary and exhausted in God's work – so often with very little result – just to serve God as we think we should. Then, suddenly, we witness a miracle and everything changes. This is just what happened to me in Luton (as I explained in Chapter 1), when God spoke to me, stopping me in my busy schedule for Him, and then sending me a greater revival because I listened and obeyed. We must begin with a healthy spiritual desire: 'Covet earnestly the best gifts' (1 Corinthians 12:31).

2 Live By God's Will

There is a Chinese legend about two men walking along the riverside. Suddenly, they hear a cry. A man is in the river struggling, and it is quite clear he is drowning. One of the passers-by said to the other, 'I cannot help him, I cannot swim, but you are a strong swimmer.' The other said nothing about the drowning man but just continued with his original conversation!

The drowning man came up again to the surface of

the river, screaming. Again, the passer-by asked his friend to save the man. Again, he ignored him. As the drowning man went under the water for the third time, the passer-by who could swim suddenly threw off his garment and dived into the river. There was a lot of turbulence as the other man watched wide-eyed from the riverside. The strong swimmer pulled the drowning man to the surface, and soon had him up the bank, pumping water from his lungs. Before long, he was sitting up recovering. The man who had watched everything said to the lifesaver, 'Why did you leave it until the very last second before saving him?' The man replied, 'I waited until he stopped struggling!'

So, too, God is waiting for our self-surrender until we stop fighting and stop struggling, and decide to live as He wants us to. As Kathryn Khulman used to say, 'Quit trying, and surrender.' There is no democracy in the Kingdom of God. It is total authoritarianism. God rules. Christ rules. The Holy Spirit dictates to us. It is for us to yield.

I was once in a meeting with the great Corrie Ten Boom. She said very little, virtually repeating the same thing over and over again. In her quiet voice, she uttered: 'There is only one way forward with the Master – surrender, surrender, surrender.' Dr Sangster calls this experience 'Making Christ truly King – not president who rules only for a while, but king who rules forever and always over you!'

Living by God's will means not cutting Him off, not walking away from the anointing, not despising what He's done for you. Jesus said, 'If any man would come after me he must deny himself, take up his cross and follow me' (Matthew 6:24). The world's opinions, habits and ways have flooded the Church – now it's time to repent and to be cleansed. When God spoke to Rees Howells in Wales and asked, 'Are you willing to become like my son, Jesus?' he was flabbergasted. He could only meekly say, 'I don't know.' God immediately replied, 'Do you want me to make you willing?'

God promised to those who love Him deeply, 'I will turn darkness into light before them, and make the rough places smooth ... I will not forsake them' (Isaiah 4:16).

3 TAKE GOD AS YOUR PARTNER

'I will teach and guide thee with mine eye ...' (Psalm 32:8). With God as our partner, we can move in miracles.

Casey Jones, a well-known business man from America, was a very godly man. He prayed about everything in a simple fashion, and he greatly prospered. His men laughed at his naïve attitude, but they greatly respected him. One day they had to move a large wooden building. They had the requisite truck and gear, but discovered they didn't have the necessary strong chain. Time did not allow them to go all the way back, but they could not do the job without this chain. With his men quietly laughing at him, Casey lifted his hands and head up to heaven in prayer: 'O God, this is your business and I forgot the chain. I'm sorry about that, Lord, but please send me a chain, you know we badly need it. Thank you, Father.'

A couple of minutes went by; then, suddenly, a small truck came up the road just past their site. It was going so fast that it had to swerve to negotiate the bends in the road. As the truck shot by something fell off the back, and all the men ran into the road to see what it was. Amazingly, they saw a huge long chain lying in the dust – and the vehicle disappearing out of sight! Casey shouted, 'Thank you, Lord, that was quick! Come on lads, what are you waiting for?' The shocked workmen got on with the job!

When we make God's thoughts our own, and ensure that He guides us, we are never beaten: 'He guided them by the skilfulness of His hands' (Psalm 78:72); 'God told Isaiah "I am the Lord thy God which teacheth thee to profit, which leadeth thee by the way thou shouldest go." '

4 PRAY UNCEASINGLY

Dr David Cho, preaching in Kuala Lumpur, Malaysia, to a crowd of 20,000 people, was asked to reveal the secret of his success. He meekly answered, 'Three things – prayer, prayer, prayer!'

Our prayers may simply be a cry from the heart, a groaning without words. Bramwell Booth, one of the Salvation Army's early leaders, said:

> It may be a few sentences wrung from the heart
> … it may be a thought or a desire lifted in a hymn
> … or a reasoned and ordered appeal from the
> mind of man to the mind of God … if only the
> soul comes into the real presence of God and
> really addresses itself to Him … that is true
> prayer and is acceptable to Him.

Often we find ourselves unable to sum our prayers up in words, like the little boy kneeling in prayer muttering 'A, B, C, D, E, F, G, H ...' His little brother heard him, and asked him what he was doing. 'Praying,' he replied. 'You're not,' retorted his brother, 'you're just repeating the alphabet.' The little lad replied, 'I don't know what to say to God, so if I repeat the letters of the alphabet God will take them and put them together into prayer for me, and then answer my prayer. He knows what I need!'

Prayer can lift your heartaches; prayer can get you through next week; prayer can meet your daily cares; prayer can resolve your impossible situations and problems. A famous American psychologist said, 'Prayer is the greatest power available to the individual in solving his personal problems, its power astonishes me.' Events take place that could only happen through the miraculous in answer to prayer. Archbishop Temple, when told by an unbeliever, 'All this prayer is coincidence' replied, 'It's funny, when I don't pray there are no coincidences, when I do pray coincidences happen.'

'Very few of God's people really pray anymore,' wrote David Wilkerson. 'Ministers especially have become so busy doing Kingdom work, there is no time to pray and even less prayer in the Congregation. We can make time for anything we really want to do. Oh, God, somehow get this generation on its knees!' The hardest lesson about praying is to stick at it. Remember the death-bed words of the great missionary Adoniram Judson, apostle to Burma: 'I never prayed sincerely and earnestly for anything, but it came. At some time, no matter how distant a day, somehow, in some shape, probably the last I should have devised, it came.'

Lindsay Glegg, the great old English preacher, when well into his 90s, told me about the rough, tough, blunt old evangelist W. P. Nicholson, who once stayed in his home. He was a rough diamond that God had marvellously changed. He was amazingly successful in drawing vast crowds, winning tens of thousands of converts. Lindsay Glegg told me his wife once went into Nicholson's bedroom to tidy up and found his bedsheets all torn into shreds! It seemed he had been wrestling with God all night and as he knelt, had obviously been tearing the sheets in his very strong hands as he prayed. No wonder he had great power from God and drew huge numbers to Christ to find new life in Him!

As you begin to pray you realize your true position in the family of God, as a citizen of the King, as a servant in the household of faith, and as a soldier in the invincible army of the King. Pray for the right things and pray right! Ask God for the right things and ask right! Miracles happen through prayer. Remember:

- Tell Him of your longings – and He will fulfil them.
- Tell Him of your temptations – and He will shield you.
- Tell Him of your wounds – and He will heal them.
- Tell Him of your discouragements – and He will get you over them.
- Tell Him of your vanity – and He will remove it.

5 FAITH FOREVER

A certain congregation complained to their minister about the church clock. It was several minutes slow, so they were leaving church a few minutes late every Sunday. The minister tried to get the clock to work properly, but had difficulties since it was so high up and tricky to reach. After various attempts he gave up. Instead, he put a notice around the clock face and when the parishioners came in the following Sunday they read, 'Don't look at my face, the problem lies deeper!'

Many people today have mislaid the key that opens the door to the Kingdom – faith. Winston Churchill said, 'I am bewildered by the world, the confusion is terrible. I attribute it in part to that great decay in belief … it's bad for a nation when it is without faith.' Some people think faith is like love – unattainable and always just out of reach – and so don't strive for it. As C. S. Lewis said, 'We live in shadowlands, where the sun is always just over the next brow of the hill, or just around the next bend in the road, it never seems to come.' But later, he was to discover a deep, renewed faith, which he expressed so beautifully in his many books.

'Faith is being sure of what we hope for and certain of what we do not see' (Hebrews 11:1). Faith musters inside of us, it is the only way to call up the treasures of God. Only faith brings us a miracle, and makes us miracle workers. Faith is a gift from God, it is the way to all the treasures of God. Faith is the greatest power in the universe given to man. Jesus prayed not that our holiness might not fail, nor that our prayer powers might not fail, nor even that our persistence might not give up. No! He prayed that *our faith might not fail* (Matthew 22:32).

Inside faith there is no defeat, outside faith there is no victory. Through faith, in spite of the dire darkness,

God is giving to believing people a great apostolic wave of revelation and power. We are living in a time like no other: God is working miracles, God is showing us He is still on the throne. The word is clear: through faith and patience we will inherit the promises.

Elisha asked Elijah for twice as much power as that shown by his master. Did he receive it? It is recorded that Elisha performed exactly twice as many miracles as did Elijah. He seemed to have more power in his dead bones than many of us have in our living bones. Faith is the programme button to get us switched on and working. As you learn faith and train your heart and mind to believe, defeatist tendencies are reversed and everything moves out of the area of the impossible into that of the possible. Remember:

- God will move heaven and earth for faith.
- God will cause the rivers to run backwards for faith.
- God will cause the sun to stand still for faith.
- God will move mountains for faith.
- God will do the impossible for his children of faith!

6 LIVE IN EXPECTATION

Many of us have lost our expectancy: every service in church is predictable, the same things happen week after week, the Holy Spirit often departs and no one misses Him. Very rarely do you find a church that astonishes you. But God promised that 'your expectation shall not be cut off' (Proverbs 23:18).

Live in the Word, live in expectation and hope. The Psalms tells us 'Those who are planted in the house of the Lord shall flourish in His courts'. A little boy said to his mum, while pointing at a cobblers repair shop, 'Jesus is in there, Mum.' She assured him that Jesus could not be in the cobblers. 'Oh yes, Mummy, look at that sign in the window!' It read 'Heeling while you wait'! What an expectation!

7 FORGET SELF

We are constantly preoccupied with ourselves. When we are consumed with what we want and what we like, we spoil everything we touch. We want – not because we need – but because we see that somebody else has. We're deceived into thinking that if other people can have certain things, we ought to have certain things also. We do not realize that having is not necessarily a guarantee of happiness.

It's time to think less of ourselves and material things, and concentrate on showing respect for others. A German schoolmaster always bowed to the boys on entering his class. Other teachers laughed at him, but he said he respected the potential God put in those boys. 'You never know what those boys may become one day,' he said. How right he was – one was Martin Luther!

Forgetting self is one of the most important factors when preparing for miracles. Paul said, 'Be devoted to one another, honour one another above yourselves, share with God's people who are in need, show hospitality ... do not be proud, be willing to associate with those in low position, do not be conceited ... do not think of yourself more highly than you ought ... but rather think of yourself with sober judgement' (Romans 12:3, 10–16).

8 Work Hard

In all my years of ministry, I have never seen a person who was greatly gifted and blessed by the Lord, who was fruitful in winning many lost souls and building up God's kingdom and church, in bringing hope, happiness and faith to society, who did not in the end become a very hard worker.

God speaks of being co-workers, how we should do our part: 'Be ye doers of the work' (James 1:25); 'Work the works of Him that sent me' (John 9:4); 'That ye might work the works of God' (1 John 6:28); 'Study the work with your own hands' (1 Thessalonians 4:11).

Never be afraid of hard work. We live in the midst of a world of trouble, turbulence, pressure and change. Trotsky said, 'The man who wanted a quiet, easy life should not have been born in the twentieth century.' The one who wants to be a success in the Kingdom of God will not achieve much without struggle, sacrifice and hard work! This is not the time for scandalous indifference and apathy. God is calling us to dedicated, hard labour. Harold Horton used to say 'God will never bless lazy bones'. So, put your hand to the plough, pull up your sleeves, and 'work, for the night cometh when no man can work' (John 9:4).

There is no substitute for work. A noted preacher tells how he and his wife took the world famous pianist, Roger Williams, to dinner in appreciation for the times he had donated his talents to their ministry. At ten o'clock Mr Williams said, 'Well, I really have to go, I must get to work.'

'Work at this time?' they asked.

'Yes, it's a rehearsal,' he said. 'I will go home and rehearse from ten o'clock 'til about two o'clock. I'll sleep for about three or four hours, and then I'll get up and rehearse for another two hours.' And he did this every day!

9 Keep a Kind Heart

Put people first: this is the foundation to allowing God to use you. Solomon said, 'The desire of a man is his kindness' (Proverbs 19:22). The basis of miracles is kindness on our lips and in our actions. Just one word of kindness can make such a difference in life!

Rudyard Kipling was visiting America, where it was estimated that his books were so popular that every published word was worth $10,000. As he left his hotel one day, a reporter shouted, 'Seeing one word from you is worth thousands of dollars, give me just one, Mr Kipling.' As he got into his taxi he called back, 'Thanks!' Famed writer Joseph Conrad said, 'Give me the right word and the right accent and by and large I will move the world.' Dreiser advocated: 'I shall pass this way but once. Therefore any good that I can do or any kindness that I can show – let me do it now. Let me not defer nor neglect it, for I shall not pass this way again.'

The key is to give of yourself. I remember Alistair Smith, a fiery Salvation Army preacher, saying 'The more you give Jesus away, the more you'll have of Him ... and the more you'll have of real life!' Or as Benjamin

Franklin put it, 'When you are best to others you are best to yourself'.

Mattern said, 'The way to happiness [is to] keep your heart free from hate, your mind from worry, live simply, give much, fill your life with love, scatter sunshine, forget self, think of others ... be kind.'

People wanting to see great signs, wonders, miracles and blessings from a divine, supernatural God cannot sometimes see what small kindnesses have to do with it, but God makes it clear – His glory is shown by lovingkindness. Miracles do indeed spring from love shown in little things and ways. There is an old Malaysian proverb: 'A bit of fragrance clings to the hand that gives the roses'.

> Kind hearts are the garden,
> Kind thoughts are the roots,
> Kind words are the blossoms,
> Kind deeds are the fruits.

10 WE OWE EVERYTHING TO JESUS

The other day a friend went to the hospital to donate blood. As he lay on his bed he noticed the man on the next bed was smiling. That mysterious smile intrigued my friend and he simply had to ask about it. 'Well,' came the reply, 'five years ago I was badly injured in a car crash. The doctors thought I'd had it. But I pulled through, and do you know what saved my life? Twenty-four pints of other people's blood.'

'But why the smile?' my friend asked.

'Because,' explained the stranger, 'today I'm giving my twelfth pint of blood, I'm halfway there and, if I'm spared, I'll pay back my debt in full.'

But my friend didn't think it at all funny. He thought it was inspiring. So do I. For perhaps a lot of us owe debts every bit as important as the stranger's, and forget to repay them. The debt we owe God is immense: our life, love, values, time, gifts, talents, character – everything!

– 15 –

Maintaining God's Blessing

> I will make them and the region around my
> hill a blessing; and I will send down the
> showers in their season; they shall be
> showers of blessing.
>
> Ezekiel 34:26

Do you recognize this scenario? You've started out on
your path with God, you've felt a real call, you've even
won converts. Your prayers have been answered, you
see the miraculous, living God working in your life, you
experience many rich blessings. But then the situation
changes. You get sidetracked. You stumble and fall,
become disheartened, get weary in well-doing. In the
end, you give up on the precious anointing which with
God has gifted you. Sound familiar? It may not have
happened to you directly, but perhaps to someone you
know. Sadly, it's an all-too-familiar story for many, and
so is something I feel is vital to address. Here, then, I've
set down fourteen essential keys to maintaining the
blessing in your walk with God. All these fourteen quali-
fications will help you to manifest God's grace with
increasing achievements and results; each, unfortu-
nately, is often lacking in many people's lives.

1 USE GOD'S GIFT REGULARLY

Niccolò Paganini (1782–1840) is perhaps the world's most famous violinist of all time. When he died he left his precious violin to his native city, making one rather curious stipulation. He specified clearly that the violin could be seen, but was never again to be played. Paganini's instrument is still on show today in a glass case. But, because it is never used, the wood is rotting. Eventually, the violin will collapse. Unless we ensure that the gift we possess is active, the body may live on, but the gift will die. If we don't watch over our gift, nurture it, cherish it or use it, then in our hour of need we may find that we haven't the resources necessary to help us.

For example, Sir Frederick Treves, surgeon to King Edward VII, was once involved in a railway accident. Happily, he escaped unhurt. The injured were laid out on the side of the track and Sir Frederick went from one to another, anxious to comfort and aid them. But as he rushed amongst them, he was heard to cry 'If only I had my instruments!' Our cry will be the same if we find that we've been neglecting our gift.

2 CLING TO GOD'S PROMISES

I wonder if you know the secret of the snowdrop? Out for a walk with my wife one day, I noticed the little green shoots of this tiny flower pushing up through the rich, dark earth. 'Do you know,' I said, 'I just can't understand how such a fragile little flower can stand up to the snow and frosts of winter.' Lilian smiled and explained. Every evening, just as dusk begins to fall, the snowdrop's head droops a little lower and its petals close. As this happens, some of the day's warmth is actually captured within the bell of the flower. So, when the night is at its coldest, the air cradled in the snowdrop's petals can be several degrees warmer than the air surrounding it and thus the flower survives.

This applies to our lives as well, for it is when life is at its coldest and darkest that we must cling to the blessings we've experienced, and hold out for the promise of the sun yet to come. 'All the promises of God are Yes and Amen' (2 Corinthians 1:20); 'He patiently endured, he obtained the promises' (Hebrews 6:15); 'Who through faith obtained the promise' (Hebrews 11:33); 'God is not slack concerning his promises' (2 Peter 3:9) – by regular reading of Scriptures such as these, you can soak your mind in God's promises, for in them is joy, confidence, hope and power.

3 Aim for the Top

A friend of ours spent a few days in the Cairngorms, in north-east Scotland. While resting and enjoying the spectacular view from one particular mountain top, he saw a young couple approaching. The girl was in a bad temper, complaining that they ought never to be climbing such a steep slope on such a hot day, that it was all the young man's fault and that she was going back down – which she did, stumbling slightly. Within minutes, our friend was joined by another couple, this time an elderly man and his wife. They both took their time about the adventure, came slowly uphill and paused regularly to admire the view and get their breath. They were chatting away to one another, and were obviously enjoying every minute. As our friend commented, it was the same steep climb and the same weather, but one party was mad, the other was glad. One failed, the other reached the top.

Doesn't this have a clear parallel to our life? It is as we lift up or visualize and reach our highest conception of God, that we become the purest, holiest and highest for Him. Some give up during the climb, but others keep going and eventually reach the heights of Him and for Him.

4 KEEP YOUR TRUST STRONG

I like this story of a mother on her way to meet her son, Donald, who had only just started school. She met an old friend on the way, who she hadn't seen for a while, and stopped for a chat. Suddenly, though, she realized she was ten minutes late. She hurried to the school gates. There wasn't a soul about, so she hurried indoors anxiously. There in the hall was Donald happily 'helping' the caretaker.

'Sorry, dear,' wailed a most contrite Mum. 'I met somebody. You weren't worried, were you?'

Donald beamed. 'No,' he said firmly. 'I knew you'd come – you said you would!' Now that's what I call trust!

These words from the Book of Habakkuk (3:17–19) are, for me, the most joyful affirmation of divine sovereignty one can possibly read anywhere:

> *Though the fig tree does not bud, and there are*
> *no grapes on the vines, though the olive crop fails*
> *and the fields produce no food, though there are*
> *no sheep in the pen and no cattle in the stalls; yet*
> *I will rejoice in the Lord, I will be joyful in God*
> *my Saviour. The sovereign Lord is my strength.*

We can best summarize the attitude of Habukkuk by asking some questions. Do we doubt? Are we troubled by the silence of God? Do we doubt because of disappointments? Do problems confuse us? Somebody has said that, given the world we live in, if God is God He is not good – and if God is good He isn't God. This shows a very shallow understanding of who God is, but that is where many people are. They have doubts. If you have doubts, will you wait? Will you wait on God and trust in Him?

5 KEEP A THANKFUL SPIRIT

There's more than a smile in this story of a five-year-old boy who, for the first time in his life, was taught at school to say grace before meals.

At home one day at dinner, he bowed his head, clasped his hands and repeated the children's grace: 'Thank you for the food we eat.' His father, who had little time for such things, was shocked. 'Now you listen to me,' he said grimly, 'I'm the one who pays for this food, so you should be thanking me, not God!'

The boy said nothing. At dinner the next day, however, he bowed his head again. 'Thank you, Daddy, for my food,' he began, 'And thank you, God, for my Daddy!'

Again and again in the Scriptures we are urged to thank God for His goodness: 'I will magnify Him with thanksgiving' (Psalm 9:30); 'I will come before Him with thanksgiving' (Psalm 95:2); 'I thank my God always' (1 Corinthians 1:4). It is good to keep praising, praying and thanking!

6 WATCH THE SMALL THINGS ...

J. R. Tolkien began creating a story for children back in the 1930s. Its first line began: 'In a hole in the ground there lived a hobbit ...' From that small beginning came that world-famous book, *The Hobbit*, and then the series, *The Lord of the Rings*, and many more which would thrill the world and reach 100 million readers around the globe.

A man I read about told how as a boy he lived in Brazil for a time. It was a long time ago, but he still remembered with affection the family cook. One day, the cook found him kneeling on the sandy garden path, stroking a snake only four inches long. The cook's eyes almost started out of his head. He reacted immediately, pushing the child towards the safety of the kitchen, shouting 'Run!'

He obeyed, and the cook later explained: 'If you see a big, large snake, you can see them coming and so can move away fast – in that way, you won't be hurt. But that small snake – well, he was so small it was hard to spot him, wasn't it? And you weren't scared of him, were you? But he was just as dangerous! If he had bitten you, you could have died!'

So it is with us: we recognize the huge serpent for what it is, but the small snake seems harmless until it is too late. Material things, lack of honesty, false ambition – they can all creep up on us and dethrone God and His power. There is a story of a businessman whose love of money was ruining his life. One day he called on his minister and argued with him about a point he had made in his sermon. The minister, who knew his visitor's failing, opened a Bible, pointed to the word 'God' and asked, 'Can you see that?'

'Of course I can,' was the impatient reply.

The minister took a penny and placed it over the word. Then he asked, 'Can you see it now?' The businessman was silenced!

Many years ago in a black township in South Africa, a young lad was with his mother when a white priest passed them by. The white priest raised his hat to the boy's mother. The lad was stunned – he had never seen any white person treat his mother with respect before. Soon after that the young boy was in hospital for twenty months. Each week that same priest came and visited him and consequently he came to a committed Christian faith and is now the Archbishop of Cape Town, Desmond Tutu. The white priest was Archbishop Trevor Huddleston. The hat being raised might have seemed a simple act but it acknowledged someone else's worth. It's a good story to remind us to live consistent lives even in the smallest of things – we never know what their impact can be.

7 NEVER LOSE SIGHT
OF SOCIETY'S NEED

You will always have power if you keep close to people's need, because God will match the challenge with the grace to meet the need. 'If I have a great need of Christ, I have a great Christ to meet my need,' so the old saying goes.

Sometimes we don't recognize people's needs around us. I recall the story of a woman who lived in a very pleasant part of town and who didn't seem to have any worries. One spring evening, when the gardens were a picture and folk were enjoying a foretaste of summer, a neighbour met her when walking along the avenue. They chatted, and everything seemed fine. The woman waved at a girl on her way to tennis, and admired someone's tulips in their front lawn. Ten minutes later, she drowned herself in the nearby river ... That woman walked in the sunshine to her death. Suppose somebody she met had been quick enough to detect the hidden despair and persuaded her to come in and have a cup of tea. Such a little thing might have accomplished so much. But they did not see her despair and heartache.

Recently at the Keswick convention I heard of a Christian who was buying an ice cream just outside the main marquee. He asked the ice cream man, 'Are you saved?' The man replied, 'I don't think I am, but it's nice of you to enquire after me. I've parked my van here outside this convention for the last 20 years, and I must have sold ice creams to thousands of people, but no one has ever asked me that question!' That Christian was certainly aware of the needs of those around him!

So many people today are desperate in their needs. They are longing for a helping, loving hand, for a Christ-glorifying message, for God's words of comfort, strength, upliftment, peace and release to be delivered by us.

8 Do Not Misjudge Others

'Don't judge a book by its cover', so the saying goes. And it's so true, isn't it? I remember holding a crusade in Blackpool some ten years ago. I re-opened a mission hall that had closed down. It soon was packed to the rafters once more, as people flocked to my services. Many were healed by the power of the Holy Spirit.

I asked my denominational headquarters to send a young, potential pastor to take care of this new-found flock after I had moved on. When I met the young man they appointed, he looked like a schoolboy. 'How on earth can this fellow do anything?' I thought. 'He's so young, so immature, he hasn't any experience, and he has all these converts to take care of!' After the crusade had finished, I reluctantly left the thriving new congregation to the new young boy. Some five years later I had an invitation to return for the anniversary celebration of the church. How amazed I was to find a thriving body of over 200 people, as well as a new branch church. The pastor is now running his own Bible School! I was pleasantly surprised, and rebuked myself at my earlier lack of insight. You can never tell the light that there is in others, the wisdom, the potential!

I think this story sums it up beautifully. It's an incident which took place in Bournemouth. An elderly couple entered a restaurant to have a bite to eat. The only two seats left were next to two punk rockers with brightly coloured hair. Their appearance was somewhat daunting to the couple, and they were a little nervous to say the least, but eventually sat down. When the waitress came the couple ordered cups of tea and two iced buns. Not long afterwards, the two youths finished off their big dinner and left. After a few minutes the waitress set down two big plates of meat, vegetables and potatoes before the old couple.

'No, no, Miss,' they said, 'you've made a mistake.' The girl smiled.

'When those two lads left,' she said, 'they told me to see you had a proper dinner and they paid for it in advance.'

The old couple looked at each other, too overcome to speak. They then quietly explained it was their golden wedding anniversary that day. They had come to Bournemouth to celebrate, but couldn't afford a cooked meal. The punks, in many people's eyes, may have looked a sight but their thoughtfulness gave an old couple their most precious memory of a golden day.

9 NEVER TIRE OF REAL PRAYER

Sir Walter Scott wrote many of his books to pay off a debt incurred by the publishing house of which he was a partner. The task was monumental. However, despite ultimately undermining his strength, it was to bring him great fame. He often related how, in all his anxiety, he would renew his strength and find calm when, after dinner, he would stroll down the garden to the home of his coachman and listen to this humble Scot raise his voice in leading his family in nightly worship.

In all the restlessness of our times, strength for the day may be found in that brief hour of prayer. These words are simply marvellous:

> There is a place where Thou canst touch the eyes
> Of blinded men to instant perfect sight:
> There is a place where Thou canst say, 'Arise!'
> To dying captives, bound in chains of night.
> There is a place where Thou canst reach the store
> Of hoarded gold and free it for the Lord:
> There is a place upon some distant shore
> Where thou canst send the worker and the Word:
> There is a place where heaven's resistant power
> Responsive moves to thine insistent plea:
> There is a place – a silent trusting hour
> Where God Himself descends and fights for thee.
> Where is that secret place?
> Dost thou ask where?
> O soul, it is the secret place of prayer!

On the way home from church one Sunday a young man remarked to the minister, 'It's all right you talking about the voice of God and the voice of conscience. Well, I must admit I've never once heard any such voice.'

'I believe you,' was the reply. 'But I sometimes wonder if the reason why many folk don't hear the voice of God is because they're making too much noise themselves.'

Maybe if you and I were quiet now and then, very quiet for just a few minutes, we might hear the voice of

God telling us what to do and assuring us of strength to do it.

10 KEEP THE WORD

Did you know that the phrase 'thus saith the Lord, God has spoken' occurs thousands of times in the Old Testament alone?

Dr E. V. Rieu, an agnostic, once translated the Scriptures into modern English. He said that he found it 'extraordinarily alive' and that it had changed him totally. Coleridge, the poet, said, 'I believe the Bible is God's word, because it finds me!' You see, Scripture makes God real to us. As Erasmus said in the fifteenth century: 'It makes Christ so real, as if He stood before my eyes.'

The greatest intercessors and prayer warriors have been those filled with the Word of God. John Bunyan said during those lonely years of exile, the only thing he wanted was his Bible. By reading the Bible daily, we too can keep God's Word alive to us and therefore make Him alive to us as well. God's Word gives us victory, it gives us life!

11 BEAT DISCOURAGEMENT

Perhaps some of the main reasons why many men and women quit their journey with God are those concerning discouragement: from other Christians who will not grasp the vision; from a secularized society that is so indifferent; from impatience with God's timing; from extreme trials, etc. These can all sap someone's energy, cause doubt, resignation; ultimately, perhaps, even depression and breakdown. With perseverance, however, we can succeed.

A nervous little boy whose family were forced out of their home when he was seven years old had to work to help support them. But the misfortune didn't end there: his mother died when he was nine; at 22 he lost his job as a shop clerk; at 23 he became a partner in a small shop, but his business partner died leaving him a huge debt which took him years to repay; at 28 the woman he loved refused to marry him; two years later he had a nervous breakdown; at 41 his four-year-old son died; at 49 he failed in his second attempt to lead the Senate of the USA; he was despised by multitudes, misunderstood, had periods of deep depression, was snubbed, ignored, laughed at. When he was 56 he was gunned down and died in a tiny anteroom. Yet one of the most famous memorials in the world is built to him in Washington DC. His name? Abraham Lincoln!

Despite the numerous hardships life threw at him, he was able to save the Union in the Civil War and set about the emancipation of slaves in the last few years of his life, thus marking him as one of the greatest US presidents. So how did he beat discouragement?

One night a friend of his was staying with him in the White House and happened to catch a glimpse of him through an open door kneeling before an open Bible. He heard him say, 'O thou great God, who heard Solomon in the night when he prayed and cried for wisdom, hear me. I cannot guide these people, I cannot guide the affairs of this country without Thy help. O Lord, hear me and save this nation.' He learned to wait for God in prayer, and the Union was preserved. His trials turned him into a great man. It's a good example for us to follow!

12 KEEP ON GOING!

John Bunney lives opposite a bowling green. One day as a visiting party waited for their bus, John strolled over to chat with them. He noticed that an old couple, well over eighty years old, looked tired, so he asked them if they'd like to step over to his house for a cup of tea. Soon they were chatting as if they'd known one another all their lives. It turned out that the old man was a keen gardener, and was especially proud of his tomatoes. He'd grown them for years, and always had an excellent crop. The old man explained his secret: 'Next time you plant your tomatoes make sure you press the soil down hard on top of them. You see, *the harder it is for the plants to come up, the stronger and better they'll be.*'

This story wonderfully reflects life: those who have known difficulty and setbacks not only stand firm throughout life's storms, but often bear the better fruit. 'If at first you don't succeed ...' – how many of us have given up in despair after a few attempts to do something, and have marked this quotation down as mere nonsense? Well, this tale shows that persistance and perseverance pay off!

Joseph Lister (1827–1912), a Glaswegian doctor, made a medical discovery that was to be of supreme importance. In 1864, 45 out of every 100 patients who underwent operations did not live – blood poisoning simply could not be cured. In August 1865, a lad called Jimmy Greenlees was brought to Lister with a badly broken leg. Although he treated the boy with kindness, Lister knew he would almost certainly die from blood poisoning. But Lister had worked for years against great difficulties to find the answer. Now, despite the sneers of others, he decided to put it to the test on Jimmy. It was simple carbolic – the first antiseptic ever to be used. And, praise be, Jimmy lived! The miracle of the antiseptic was proved beyond a shadow of a doubt and the whole course of medicine was changed because he persisted. Lister was showered with the highest honours. But he could never know that millions all over the world would owe their lives to him in the years to come and, as is inscribed on his grave, that 'all generations would call him blessed'. As Winston Churchill said: 'Cost and sorrow will be the companion of our journey, hardship, constancy and valour our shield. We must be undaunted, inflexible.'

13 GUARD YOUR TONGUE

Sir Thomas Beecham, the great English conductor, when asked about the British people and music, replied, 'The English don't care much about music, but they like the noise it makes.' Could that equally apply to our words? The uncontrolled tongue has been called 'the devil's bellows', so use your words wisely.

Let your words be few unless they are positive, kind words. Sir Billy Butlin, showman and wealthy businessman, gave thousands of pounds away to charity. Although regularly in the public eye, he did not care for public speeches; he used to say, 'I have only two speeches: a short one – "thank you" – and a long one – "thank you very much!" ' Have tact, like the boss who said carefully to one of his employees who had been slacking a lot, 'Son, I don't know how we are going to get by without you, but starting on Monday we're going to try!'

Reflect on these words from Proverbs 14:3: 'The lips of the wise shall preserve them …'

14 ABOVE ALL ELSE, LOVE

I see my calling in life, my ministry of the Holy Spirit, as one of love, love and more love … a work of love, a walk of love, a life of love, a labour of love. Over 25,000 letters a year arrive at our office in Chippenham, Wiltshire. Many are from desperately sick people, many write and say, 'Thank you for your love for us'. Seeing the love of Christ inspires and motivates us; it certainly did for the man in this true story.

If you ever are lucky enough to visit the Isle of Mull off the west coast of Scotland, make sure you take a boat trip out around the cliffs, for there you will see written the great Bible text 'God is love'. The story goes that a father and daughter, whilst on a visit to Mull, were strolling along the cliff-top path when the child tripped and tumbled over the precipice. Terrified, the father raced down the path to the beach, telling himself that no one could survive such a fall. Yet to his amazement he found his daughter alive, and only slightly hurt. That day, after taking her home, he went back to the cliff-face with paint and a brush and at the spot where she had fallen he painted the text, 'God is Love'. He believed only a miracle had saved his child. He asked the crew of the mailboat servicing Mull to renew the message from time to time, so that all who came and went would see it. And today, years later, these men are still keeping their word, for the message is still there, proclaiming a father's faith to all who pass.

God loves us so much, we must endeavour to love others and bring them to His love as He desires us to. I wish that we could all be like this little girl, Sarah, talking to her aunt. 'Suppose you could have a wish,' Aunt Ida suggested. 'what would you ask for?'

'An old doll,' Sarah replied.

'Wouldn't you rather have a new one?'

'Oh no, I'd like an old doll. See, new dolls get loved a lot, but old dolls get thrown on one side and forgotten. I'd like an old doll who wanted somebody to love her – and I'd love her and love her and love her!'

Love makes all things bright – the hard task, the poor home, the daily chores, loss of money, disappointments. Love turns the commonest stuff of life to gold. We sometimes put a small X at the foot of a letter to someone we love. The Christian knows it was on a real cross that love was fully revealed. I'll end with this verse, which encapsulates for me what God's love is about:

God's love is like a circle of an eternity ring,
A circle big and round,
And when you see a circle,
See that no ending can be found.
And so the love of Jesus goes eternally,
Forever and forever I know God loves me.

– 16 –

PRAISE HIM!

> The Lord has done this, and it is marvellous
> in our eyes. This is the day the Lord has
> made; let us rejoice and be glad in it.
> > PSALM 118:23–24

This glorious text from the Book of Psalms always reminds me of a man I greatly admire. He's called Don, and he's from Cork, Ireland. A writer and adventurer, and a devout Roman Catholic, he truly has experienced a personal encounter with Christ.

Don came to help out at one of our crusades in Dublin. He worked with me for four days, in which hundreds crowded our meetings. He was intrigued at so many people rushing forward to find Christ, and witnessed it as a great moving of the Holy Spirit and something for which he had prayed to take place in Ireland over many years. He was thrilled.

After my time in Ireland, I preached in Europe for a short while, then returned to Wiltshire. Almost immediately after arriving at the office, I received a call from one of our crusade organizers in County Kildare. He told me the tragic news that Don's second youngest son, who had come to know Christ personally in one of my meetings, had died in a car accident. He had been walking home from a service when someone offered him a lift, so he got in. Somehow, the car careered off the road, and Don's son was terribly injured in the crash. Medics rushed to the scene, and frantically tried to save him. As he lay on the roadside, his last words to the nurse were: 'I'm not afraid to go. I have no fear of death'.

At the huge funeral, Don stood and preached to the crowds, although he was griefstricken. He spoke softly and firmly about the personal miracle that was sustaining him at such an hour – that miracle was the knowledge of Christ's love shining through even the darkest hour. Sometimes it's hard to fathom how Don, or anyone in a time of great sadness, could still reach out to, find and praise Christ.

I Don't Feel Like Praising God

Many believers have run out of resources or manifestations. They are looking for glorious feelings, a special joy, but simply don't feel them. It is at such times that they give up.

Perhaps the Bible can help at these moments. It isn't a psychology textbook, but it gives us the wisest counsel for experiencing happiness here and now. Proverbs 17:22, for example, assures us that 'a merry heart does good, like medicine, but a broken spirit dries the bones'. The writers of the psalms urge their readers to make praise a way of life. The Psalmist wrote: 'From the rising of the sun unto the going down of the same the Lord's name is to be praised' (Psalm 133:3). Scripture reminds us that even when *we* don't feel anything, it doesn't mean that God doesn't! The Psalmist wrote, 'Lord, you have examined me and know me, you know everything I do ... you see me resting and working ... in fact, even before I speak you know what I will say' (Psalm 139:1–5).

The ancient community of Qum'ran, where the Dead Sea Scrolls were discovered, made it clear that praise is not something that rests on our changes of mood. Manual 10 of the Qum'ran Rule of discipline says: 'As long as I live it shall be a rule engraved on my tongue to bring praise like a fruit for an offering, and my lips as a sacrificial gift.'

There is a secret to getting through and praising God even when you don't feel in the mood. Reach out to the Lord. Catch a fresh glimpse of His majesty and power. Regain a right perspective on who He is and who you are. His love and presence are the foundation which never moves.

He is the place where broken hearts are healed. He is the place where the heavy load of sin is lifted. He is the place where the torture of worry is resolved. He is the place where marching orders are received and the way ahead discovered. He is the place where indescribable joy is found! Some of us can go for days, months or even years without entering the holy place. We can maintain a regular prayer time, be frequent at worship and remain constant in Bible study. But we have not moved past the wall of our indifference to the holy place of His awesome presence.

Today, move beyond the walls of apathy which shut you out. The curtain is torn in two ... the way is clear. You have access through Jesus Christ to enter the holy place – the most wonderful place of all.

It's significant that our Saviour said on several occasions, 'Be of good cheer' (Matthew 9:2, 22; 14:27; Acts 23:11). In full view of life's many crises, He encourages us with this word of reassurance; 'Be of good cheer, I have overcome the world' (John 16:33). No matter what happens, you can be happy in the Lord.

In Deeper Reverence, Praise

Dr Daniel Mark, a heart specialist at Duke University, USA, recently carried out extensive research on the effect of feelings of happiness and optimism on his patients. The *New York Times* article on his work was headed 'Optimism Can Mean Life for Heart Patients and Pessimism Death'. The article begins with these words: 'A healthy outlook helps heal the heart.' Faith in God can produce this kind of feeling, and people who look beyond their present difficulty and put their trust in God's goodness cannot help but be joyful and ready to praise. Teilhard de Chardin summed up the experience when he wrote: 'Radiant word, Blazing Power, you mould the manifold so as to breathe your life into it, I pray you, lay on me your hands. Powerful and considerate, omnipresent, which plunge into the depths of the totality of my being through all that is most profound.'

Time and again in Scripture we read of people praising God after they have experienced victory. For example, when the Israelites won a great victory over the Canaanite King Jabin, they praised the Lord. Deborah and Barak, the leaders of the people, worshipped together the great God who had given them victory. The original text shows us that they literally knelt down before Him and gave thanks.

We, too, should have this attitude of reverence. When we praise him, we remember that we are in the presence of the Almighty, and so can approach him only with humility.

One afternoon I attended sung evensong in Bath Cathedral. As the April sunshine streamed in through the stained-glass windows, and the beautiful harmony of the choir filled the sanctuary, I sensed the presence of the Lord and knelt in adoration. I was kneeling because my heart was bowed before Him, and I was overwhelmed by a wonderful sense of His majesty and glory.

Even if we are not in a praising mood, it helps to kneel before God and await His presence. It means we are creating space in our lives for silence, meditation, reflection and inner peace. This happened to a minister friend of mine on a youth weekend. It was nearly midnight, and he and the young people, were in a large field gazing up at the moon and the stars. It had been a very long day, my friend was tired, and wasn't exactly in a praising mood. But he says that a stillness descended around the group as they looked up into the sky. They sang that wonderful hymn, 'Be still and know that I am God', and he remembers immediately feeling ready to praise.

A pastor friend told me of the visit of some youth evangelists to his church. 'Every morning, I joined them for their devotional session in the local park. I'll never forget their commitment to praising the Lord, even when they were tired, or their mission wasn't going well. Praise was a part of who they were.'

NOT INFERIOR, BUT SUPERIOR!

The story goes of a man who complained to a psychiatrist about having an inferiority complex. The doctor listened patiently, then said, 'The good news is, you don't have a complex. The bad news is, you are inferior!'

Gideon was a lot like that man. He was an unlikely candidate for national leadership. He never dreamed of leading Israel to a military victory over its enemies. But the Lord called him to a task that required great courage and leadership. He pushed aside Gideon's plea of inadequacy. 'Go in this might of yours,' He said. 'Have I not sent you?' (Judges 6:14). God would equip him; Gideon's responsibility was simply to obey. Remember, God's resources are always equal to His requirements.

I remember a story about a woman who was very discouraged because of the many problems in her life. As she was walking down the street, she met a fellow believer who asked, 'How are you doing today?' With a sour look and a bitter shrug she replied, 'Oh, not too bad – under the circumstances.' The other person quickly countered, 'Well, get *above* the circumstances! That's where Jesus is.'

You can beat the bad feelings and begin to know good feelings. No guilt, shame, fear, remorse, regret or recrimination will trouble you – it's so fantastic, so fabulous, so fulfilling to have the forgiveness and peace of Jesus Christ in your heart ... it is a wellspring of enthusiasm, optimism and creativity. When you're alive with the power of Jesus, praise will flow naturally.

These prayers, said daily, can help you combat negative feelings and let positive ones shine through:

> *Lord, make my life a window for your light to shine through and a mirror to reflect your love to all I meet.* Amen.

> *Oh Lord, I see a leaf on the wave. Oh Lord, I see a feather in the wind. Oh Lord, I see a little white cloud in the breeze. Oh Lord, you be the wave – I'll be the leaf. Oh Lord, you be the wind – I'll be the feather. Oh Lord, you be the breeze, I'll be the little white cloud.* Amen.
>
> ROBERT SCHULLER

Soon you'll be praising God saying:

> The negative moods and thoughts were
>   unmerciful, but I climbed above them!
> The setbacks were painful, but I bounced back,
> The therapy was rough, but I got through it.
> The scrutiny was scorching but I came out clean.
> I'm an undergoer who became an overcomer!

J. Namath wrote a book titled *I Can't Wait Until Tomorrow … 'Cause I get Better Looking Every Day*. As egotistical as that sounds, it can help us see how we – believers in the Lord Jesus Christ – should view ourselves in the lifelong process of becoming like Him. Our joy increases with our daily walk with God.

Frederick Myconius was very sick and about to die. He wrote a farewell letter to his dear friend Martin

Luther, who sent back this response: 'I command you in the name of God to live because I still have need of you in the work of reforming the Church … The Lord will never let me hear that you are dead, but will permit you to survive me. For this I am praying, this is my will, and may my will be done, because I seek only to glorify the name of God.' Myconius, who had become too weak to talk, regained his strength and outlived Luther by two months.

The poignant words of the verse below capture precisely how sometimes we don't feel as if we can praise God, and become discouraged, but then are suddenly able to and once more regain our vigour and strength. With a renewed confidence and greater positivity, we will succeed.

Hallelujah!
I ran through fields of green,
I raced until the air rushed past my face.
The clean air filled my lungs, I yelled for joy.
The cares of years had rolled away,
I held my head up high.
The weight upon my soul had gone.
Free at last – I knew that Jesus was alive,
Running with me
Living in my heart.
The Lord was with me in that moment of ecstatic
     living.
The fear had gone.
The frustrations of a lifetime blown away.
Free at last –
Nothing in this world or the next could ever

Bind me down again.
The Lord had set me free!
But that was yesterday.
I just don't feel that way right now.
I'm just not in that praising mood.
The sky is grey and dark again today
My work has got me down,
I'm tired ...
And you seem far away.
But I remember yesterday ...
... I raise my head again.
I praise you Lord.

I'd like to end by sharing a very personal story with you, one that shows how in the midst of despair, when it seems that there's nothing but misery and helplessness, the power of prayer can work miracles and God once more can be praised.

I was born in Chippenham, deep in the lovely Wiltshire countryside, to a loving, caring family. My mother was a wonderful, faithful lady. My grandmother was one of those fortunate enough to be blessed in that last great revival to sweep our people – the 1904 Welsh revival. I remember, as a tiny boy, my *great*-grandmother, a Calvinist Methodist, pouring over her Bible when she was well into her 80s. So I was surrounded by faith from the moment I arrived!

One dreadful day, though, when I was two and a half years old, I fell into the river at Upton, in Weston-Super-Mare. When they fished me out I had no heartbeat and wasn't even breathing. My mother didn't know what else to do but pray. So she sought God with all the prayer power she could muster, and after some minutes – although she said later it felt like a lifetime – my pulse began again and life flooded back into me. The sheer strength of her prayer worked a miracle!

Later, at four years of age, I was struck down with pneumonia; in those days, you must remember, there was generally little hope for children who succumbed to such a fatal, sinister sickness. My mother placed me in my cot by the log fire downstairs, since the advice from our new Canadian doctor was to keep me as warm as possible. However, he was not at all positive about my future. 'I'm afraid there's nothing we can do,' he told my mother. 'I will be writing out a death certificate for him tomorrow.' (Doctors were certainly far more blunt in those days!) Mother's tears flowed all night. Looking back, I can just about remember the fever and the heavy blankets, but I know that there will have been prayers and love surrounding me. What I *do* remember, though, is so vivid and real to me that it still lives with me all these years later. There, in front of the fire, I saw in the darkness a great castle approaching, coming nearer and nearer towards me. It looked like a great white castle, or as I realize now – years later – more like a city. It was a truly magnificent sight, but it suddenly vanished – just like that, almost like the wave of a wand.

The next morning, my mother tells me, I was sitting up, eating my hot porridge cheerfully – in the best of health. There were no tears, only smiles, laughter and rejoicing. The doctor arrived expecting to be met with woe, cries, screams, sadness and sorrow, but instead found people joyfully giving thanks to God.

Exhilaration filled our home as praise was offered again and again to God. As John Blanchard puts it: 'When the world is on top of you – PRAY, when you are on top of the world – PRAISE!'

PRAISE IN PRAYER WILL BRING YOU:
from being bitter to being better
from indifference to decisiveness
from resisting to receiving
from destroying to developing
from aimlessness to priorities
from irresponsibility to accountability
from being spiritually disabled to being spiritually
    enabled
from giving up to getting up
from blending in to standing out
from a jawbone to a backbone
from a slowboat to a showboat
from a 'wanna be' to a 'gonna be'
from drifting through life to steering through life
from problems to solutions
from more of everything to more of God!

The light shines in darkness, and the darkness did not overcome it.

JOHN 1:5

– 17 –

PRAYER POWER

Use this powerful list of the real results prayer can bring to give you strength and comfort at all times in life.

- When despite your best efforts, life seems fruitless – *the power of prayer will help bring new growth*.
- When fatigue sets in and you feel you've lost direction – *the power of prayer will give you the energy to get back on the right path*.
- When your dreams appear to evaporate into smoke – *the power of prayer will give you new hope*.
- When you've lost the will to fight or continue – *the power of prayer will fill you with renewed strength*.
- When you can't recall the wonders that God has done – *the power of prayer will bring them fresh into your life*.
- When your words and deeds are misunderstood – *the power of prayer will help you to resolve any awkwardness*.
- When the sun never seems to shine – *the power of prayer will fill you with the rays of God's love*.
- When you're told that you'll never amount to anything – *the power of prayer will give you the courage to fight back*.
- When sorrow and grief overwhelm you – *the power of prayer will ease your troubled mind*.

- When you've lost every reason for living – *the power of prayer will keep that last bit of hope alive.*
- When your praising spirit feels empty and your heart is hollow – *the power of prayer will inspire you to rejoice once more.*
- When it feels as if the world is on your shoulders – *the power of prayer will ease your burden.*
- When the darkness never seems to go away – *the power of prayer will allow that first chink of light to enter.*
- When everything you touch seems to fail and disappear – *the power of prayer will help you carry on.*
- When you're at your lowest ebb and you don't feel appreciated by anyone – *the power of prayer will give you a new sense of worth.*
- When you understand the promises of God, but can't see them in day-to-day living – *the power of prayer will help you have faith and trust again.*
- When you aim to do your best, but the target keeps moving away – *the power of prayer will get you back on track.*

I pray that you may experience what I have felt, seen and known in recent times – miracles galore and multitudes rehabilitated, all by the wonderful works of Jesus Christ. I love to express this in J. R. R. Tolkien's words: '[When Frodo] smelt a sweet fragrance on the air … it seemed to him as a dream, the grey rain turned to silver glass and was rolled back, and he beheld white shores, and beyond them a far green country under a swift sunrise …' That's the final effect of prayer power!

LEARNING MORE OF GOD'S POWER

Due to the overwhelming response of thousands to the present awakening in the United Kingdom, through the commitment to God's guidance of the Rev. Melvin Banks, his family and their team, he personally or one of his family would be happy to make themselves available to visit your town, city, suburb, church or fellowship, in order to share these amazing stories and testimonies. Please contact the address given below.

The Rev. Melvin Banks welcomes letters, invitations and prayer requests for you or your loved ones.

Also available are videos, audio tapes and free literature. For the latest news of the Revival send a stamped addressed envelope to:

The Rev. Melvin Banks
International Crusade Office
44 Monks Way
Chippenham
Wiltshire
SN15 3TT
England
Telephone: (01249) 655712